“Nietzsche is not our judge, but we should let him take the witness stand. Yet what do we do when the philosopher’s enigmatic testimony amounts to a powerful judgment against us? Michael McEwen offers a gift of interpretation, offering Nietzsche space to speak while excavating the philosopher’s pervasive influence on the modern cultural imagination. In response, McEwen commends a public theology that is clear-eyed, irenic, and hopeful, insisting that after all has been heard, Christianity’s story is more capacious than Nietzsche’s parodies, and that the weakness of God is still stronger than men.”

—**Justin Ariel Bailey**, professor of theology, Dordt University

“For many Christians, if they read Nietzsche at all it is often for the predetermined purpose of simply proving him wrong. By contrast, McEwen models how to read Nietzsche’s texts as a Christian in a way that is not only fruitful but virtuous.”

—**Amber Bowen**, assistant professor of philosophy, Eastern University

“Our inability to see, understand, and engage the intellectual forces that shape us has a devastating effect on our lives and witness. In that light, McEwen’s work *The Devil Reads Nietzsche* is a welcomed addition to the field for helping us engage these intellectual forces while also trying to be faithful to Christ.”

—**Jamie Dew**, president, New Orleans Baptist Theological Seminary

“In this erudite volume, McEwen expertly analyzes Nietzsche’s thought and his philosophical milieu, while simultaneously interpreting contemporary American culture in light of those ideas. His goal, though, is not merely to explain but to disciple—to instruct readers how to view their own cultural context and philosophical inheritance through the lens of the gospel of Jesus Christ and his inspired Word. I highly recommend this important book."

—**Matthew Emerson**, dean of theology, arts, and humanities and professor of religion, Oklahoma Baptist University

"It's high time Christians take Nietzsche seriously—not in the sense that they see him as grave opponent or a high-water mark of anti-Christian belief. Rather, they need to take his questions and categories seriously and really listen to what he says and why. Why must they do that? As Michael McEwen aptly shows in this accessible book, Nietzsche's nihilism haunts every crevice of our culture. He inherits a German philosophical tradition that turns all knowledge inward on the self, cutting us off from both God and his very real world. If you want to know why so much of our culture is marked by chaos, McEwen's charitable reading of Nietzsche is a helpful guide. To grow in love for God and your neighbor, read this book."

—**Dennis Greeson**, dean of the Alexandrian Institute

"Here is a clear-eyed and even charitable reading of Nietzsche, read by someone within the community of faith—a community Nietzsche himself despised. For those who find him bewildering and perhaps offensive but still want to understand Nietzsche, McEwen serves as a steady guide. Find out how Nietzsche's message of liberation resulted in bondage and why the modern world found it so attractive."

—**Kenneth Keathley**, research professor of theology, Southeastern Baptist Theological Seminary

"Serious engagement with Nietzsche is not for the faint of heart, for his opposition to Christianity and his piercing cultural critiques demand the most careful reflection and thoughtful refutation. Too many have dismissed Nietzsche outright, but McEwen has taken up the bold task of engaging Nietzsche's thought with a view to both what can we learn, but also what we must reject according to God's truth. As McEwen rightly points out, Nietzsche's audacious rejection of morality and metaphysics, and his declaration of the 'death of God' garners him a provocative hearing. But is it a sustainable view of the world or way of life? McEwen capably dissects and diagnoses Nietzsche's claims, admitting keen insights at points while also demonstrating falsehood and incoherence at others. Ultimately, McEwen draws upon Nietzsche's work to point readers to the better, more beautiful, and true story of the world that finds its center in the Lord Christ. Very well written and highly recommended."

—**Benjamin T. Quinn**, director, L. Russ Bush Center for Faith and Culture and associate professor of theology, Southeastern Baptist Theological Seminary

The Devil Reads Nietzsche

The Devil Reads Nietzsche

A **PUBLIC THEOLOGY** *for the* **POST-CHRISTIAN AGE**

Michael McEwen

B&H
ACADEMIC®
BRENTWOOD, TENNESSEE

The Devil Reads Nietzsche: A Public Theology for the Post-Christian Age

Published by B&H Academic®
Brentwood, Tennessee

ISBN: 978-1-4300-9562-0

Dewey Decimal Classification: 230.01
Subject Heading: CULTURE \ THEOLOGY \ CHRISTIANITY

Cover design by Emily Keafer Lambright. Cover image: Saint James the Less, defaced by Iconoclasts, St Michael's Church, Irstead, Norfolk UK. Sourced from ASP Religion/Alamy.

Printed in the United States of America
30 29 28 27 26 25 VP 1 2 3 4 5 6 7 8 9 10

To my four children: Garland, Ezra, Sophie, and Ava.
May you learn to disagree charitably and
compassionately with your neighbors.

CONTENTS

Part One

Promises

Part 1 of this project has a threefold aim. First, it will introduce you to Friedrich Nietzsche and acclimate you to the life, terminology, and philosophical arc of this German giant. Second, it will contextualize Nietzsche's work within his European (especially German) milieu. After all, no figure—past or present—thinks, writes, desires, or imagines in a vacuum. This brief contextualization of Nietzsche will help you better grasp his life, terminology, and philosophical goals. Third, it will explicate my own personal goals for this project. In other words, I will make several promises to you on how I intend to read Nietzsche, and I will invite you to do the same.

Introduction

> *I came across this book in old Rohn's second-hand bookshop, and taking it up very gingerly I turned over its pages. I know not what demon whispered to me: 'Take this book home with you.' At all events, contrary to my habit of not being hasty in the purchase of books, I took it home. Back in my room I threw myself into the corner of the sofa with my booty, and began to allow that energetic and gloomy genius to work upon my mind. In this book, in which every line cried out renunciation, denial, and resignation, I saw a mirror in which I espied the whole world, life, and my own mind depicted in frightful grandeur.*[1]

These are the recorded words of Friedrich Nietzsche after he discovered by chance Arthur Schopenhauer's *The World as Will and Representation*. Of the numerous books that influenced Nietzsche, Schopenhauer's work is near the top of that list.

[1] Julian Young, *Friedrich Nietzsche: A Philosophical Biography* (Cambridge University Press, 2010), 81.

I highlight this quote because, like Nietzsche, I also happened to stumble unexpectedly across a volume in a bookstore (this one a Barnes & Noble) that has deeply influenced my life and thought: Nietzsche's own *Ecce Homo*. Having no history with German philosophy at the time—much less enough Latin to understand what *Ecce Homo* even translated to—I glanced at its contents and, not certain if a demon whispered in my ear as well, paid for it and took it to my apartment.

About an hour into the foreign landscape of *Ecce Homo*, I was confused yet enamored, conflicted yet curious, by its late nineteenth-century German author. Ironically, I could feel his tone without understanding most of the content of his book. In what I could understand, I suspected he was an atheist, and as such, I deduced that some of my (theologically) fundamentalist friends at the time probably would have suspected that the devil loved Nietzsche. Hence, the title of the work you are holding. Nearly two decades after perusing through *Ecce Homo*, I still find myself traversing through the thick forests of German and French philosophy.

Additionally, this book's title also finds inspiration from another academic hero of mine: James K. A. Smith and his book *The Devil Reads Derrida and Other Essays on the University, the Church, Politics, and the Arts*. In that collection of essays, Smith engages with various cultural topics while winsomely establishing a theological *pathos*, *ethos*, and *logos* for the church in its cultural moment.[2] In my early Christian walk, I heard from inside

---

[2] Generally understood, *pathos*, *ethos*, and *logos* were Greek rhetorical categories meant to develop students into competent communicators who consider emotion (*pathos*), character (*ethos*), and reason (*logos*) while speaking and in dialogue.

and outside the walls of the church that—because of my allegiance to Christ—I was in a cultural *war*, and the church should fight to demolish all anti-Christian ideas.

But I found in Smith that "every line cried out renunciation, denial, and resignation," and "I saw a mirror in which I espied the whole world, life, and my own mind depicted in frightful grandeur." Smith does not prescribe a renunciation, denial, and resignation of reality or religion per se, but rather a renunciation, denial, and resignation from a particular *cultural* Christianity—a set of Christianized ideologies that, upon sounding out with a hammer, I "hear[d] in response that famous hollow sound which speaks of swollen innards."[3] Through Smith's works, I was trained (or dare I say discipled) in how to engage with cultural ideologies, narratives, and practices from the deep recesses of a Christian intellectual tradition. With a tap of the theological hammer, I realized that the ideology of "culture wars" has predispositions in violence, revenge, fear, and hostility—all antithetical qualities of Jesus and his teachings.

Following the academic spirit of Smith, *The Devil Reads Nietzsche* has one primary aim: to disciple readers to engage with cultural ideologies from *within* the biblical-theological narrative and the Christian intellectual tradition. In this book, I intend to demonstrate such an aim through a conversation with Nietzsche and Nietzschean topics (theology, identity, meaning, morality, truth, faith, and hope) so that the church might learn how to engage with culture charitably, wisely, and winsomely.

---

[3] Quotes from Friedrich Nietzsche, *Twilight of Idols: How to Philosophize with a Hammer*, trans. Duncan Large (Oxford University Press, 1998), 3.

Reading Nietzsche Charitably *Within* the Biblical-Theological Narrative

Before we engage with Nietzsche, I wish to first clarify a few hermeneutical mechanics of my reading of him, mechanics that would have infuriated Nietzsche for many reasons. First, I am assuming the truthfulness of the Christian metanarrative. Second, I am assuming the reality of a Christian metaphysic. Finally, I am assuming the ultimate goodness of a Christian morality. In other words, to read Nietzsche in a Christian way is to reintroduce all the problems he attempted to transcend, as I will demonstrate later. Part 2 of this book will serve as an extended response to Nietzsche, but let me note two relevant points: Some of his critiques were warranted, such as "sounding out the idols" of particular theological systems in his day.

Christians generally respond to Nietzsche in one of two ways. They either *cast* him out as an atheistic leper carrying heretical diseases, or they *contrast* his philosophy with Scripture, noting all the conceptual dissimilarities and creating an impasse between the two. Rarely do Christians practice a *charitable* reading of Nietzsche that actually listens to him in order to engage thoughtfully with him. In response to the methodological insufficiencies of the two general Christian attitudes toward Nietzsche, this work will attempt to offer a charitable reading of Nietzsche.[4] However, a few clarifiers are necessary.

---

[4] We might say that we need a "deep reading" that produces a more charitable, hospitable hermeneutic: a reading that practices convictional compassion. One recent resource that thoughtfully curates a charitable, hospitable, and convictional hermeneutic is Rachel B. Griffis, Julie Ooms, and Rachel M. De Smith Roberts, *Deep Reading: Practices to*

First, a charitable reading is Other oriented.[5] People in my evangelical camp might say charity is *missional* because it seeks what is lost and broken (Luke 15). In a charitable reading, the Other is not a utilitarian means to an end but is itself enjoyed and valued. When Nietzsche is read charitably, he is sought after in order to be known and understood.[6]

In contrast, the approaches of casting out and contrasting are grounded in enmity and conflict. When enmity orients us, it tends to distance that which is foreign or Other. As August Wilson's character, Bono, in the play *Fences* states: "Some people build fences to keep people out and other people build fences to keep people in." Many Christians have fearfully built fences to keep out foreign ideas like those of Nietzsche while simultaneously insulating and protecting themselves from such strangeness. However, as Augustine aptly said: "Knowledge is valuable

Subvert the Vices of Our Distracted, Hostile, and Consumeristic Age (Baker Academic, 2024).

[5] Generally speaking, the Other in literature and philosophy is a term denoting an unbelonging person or group—a marginalized figure of difference and heteronomy.

[6] It is noteworthy to spotlight a repeated term in Luke 15, where Jesus strings together the parables of the lost sheep, the lost coin, and the lost son. That term is the verb *heuriskō*, which in Luke 15 denotes a discovery through the act of searching. Each of the "things" (sheep, coin, son) can be found only if there is a pursuer. In the parables of the shepherd and the coin, they're found while being lost; they did nothing to be discovered. Yet, there is a clear difference in the narrative concerning the parable of the lost son. He is found only because he is receptive to being discovered by the father. In connection with Nietzsche, the first two methods of casting out and contrasting are insufficient because there's a failure to intentionally search in order to discover knowingly.

only when charity informs it."[7] Perfect love casts out fear (1 John 4:18) so that we might embrace the foreignness of the Other in order to rightly know it.[8]

Second, a charitable reading practices a convictional hospitality. Loving one's neighbor does not imply that we either unclothe ourselves of our convictions or become apathetically insensitive like the priest and Levite in the parable of the Good Samaritan.[9] Rather, as Tim Keller and John Inazu write in *Uncommon Ground*: "Careful listening, sympathetic understanding, and thoughtful questioning can help us draw closer to others as we come to recognize the shared experiences that unite us and the different experiences that divide us."[10] Keller and Inazu add, "The ability to put ourselves in someone else's shoes requires humility, and the impetus for doing so requires patience rooted

---

[7] Augustine, *City of God, Volume III: Books 8–11*, trans. David S. Wiesen, Loeb Classical Library (Harvard University Press, 1957), 366.

[8] As I write this paragraph, I am reminded of Rosaria Butterfield's beautiful and timely work, *The Gospel Comes with a House Key: Practicing Radically Ordinary Hospitality in Our Post-Christian World* (Crossway, 2018). She writes, "Radically ordinary hospitality values the time it takes to invest in relationships, to build bridges, to repent of sins of the past, to reconcile. Bridge building and remaking friendships cannot be rushed" (34–35).

[9] To undress ourselves from our values and convictions is a Rawlsian myth. John Rawls believed that the hope of a more civilized and just society was attainable if we took off our core beliefs, thereby leaving everyone "neutral." He called this the "veil of ignorance" and contended that upon removing the veil, all citizens would become equal, since they would then be convictionally naked. Underneath Rawls's proposal are Enlightenment ideals of objectivity and neutrality. See Rawls, *A Theory of Justice* (Belknap, 1999).

[10] Tim Keller and John Inazu, *Uncommon Ground: Living Faithfully in a World of Difference* (Nelson, 2021), xvii.

in hope and tolerance grounded in love."[11] In no shape or form am I naively overlooking the indisputable differences between Christian Scripture and Nietzsche. Rather, when necessary, I will point those differences out while also engaging with Nietzsche from within a convictional framework of Christlike love, hospitality, patience, and hope (Rom 12:9–19).

As we begin to interpret Nietzsche, my aim is to read him charitably by being attentive to his words, tone, claims, propositions, questions, use of aphorisms and irony, and overall philosophical project.[12] If, at any moment I mute his voice, then I have failed to "seek after" him in the Lukan sense of understanding, empathy, and compassion, and if I lack understanding, empathy, and compassion, then my words are nothing more than philosophical "gongs" and "cymbals" (1 Cor 13:1).

As noted at the beginning of this section, I am assuming the truthfulness of the Christian metanarrative. Thus, echoing the method and approach of Christopher Watkin in his book *Biblical Critical Theory*, I wish to "paint a picture of humanity and of our world through the lens of the Bible and to compare

---

[11] Keller and Inazu, *Uncommon Ground*, xviii.

[12] In *The Devil Reads Derrida*, James K. A. Smith writes, "So long as we all begin from the assumption that we want to bring all of our thinking and doing under the Lordship of Christ and the light of the biblical narrative, my brothers and sisters are quite happy to hear a different take on their settled convictions—as long as it is offered in charity and humility, not with scolding and condescension." Smith, *The Devil Reads Derrida and Other Essays on the University, the Church, Politics, and the Arts* (Eerdmans, 2009), xvi. Even though Smith is writing on some cultural hot-button topics, this, too, is my hopeful temperament and aim, which is to produce a surprising reading of Nietzsche (different from what most Christians think of him) while doing so charitably and missionally.

aspects of this image to alternative visions." We might consider *The Devil Reads Nietzsche* as a focused case study of Watkin's methodological approach in *Biblical Critical Theory*. Like Watkin's work, I desire for this book to be "about how the whole Bible sheds light on the whole of life, how we can read and understand our society, our culture, and ourselves through the lens of the Bible's storyline."[13] Unlike Watkin, however, I'll be focusing his biblical-theological method upon the work of one particular thinker—Friedrich Nietzsche, one of the "alternative visions" of which he speaks.

In agreement with Watkin, a biblical-theological approach is a narration *of* or *about* the world. As John Milbank suggests, a Christian take on the world is theological, ecclesiological, and sociological, because "the Church defines itself, in its practice, as in continuity and discontinuity with [surrounding human] societies."[14] The church knows itself (and others) because the triune God—via Scripture—reveals himself to the church, thereby giving his people an interpretation of what the world is like and the church's participation in it. Scripture, we might say, unfolds a metaphysic and a morality. Watkin refers to this way of seeing the "as-structure," which is "the meaning we give to objects and events that makes us experience them in particular ways."[15] Everyone *sees as* or according to a narratival take of the world. To see without a script is to be lost and wandering, inducing a feeling of aimlessness. Yet, the church is unique in that it *sees as* or

[13] Christopher Watkin, *Biblical Critical Theory: How the Bible's Unfolding Story Makes Sense of Modern Life and Culture* (Zondervan Academic, 2022), 2.

[14] John Milbank, *Theology and Social Theory: Beyond Secular Reason*, rev. ed. (Blackwell, 2006), 382.

[15] Watkin, *Biblical Critical Theory*, 6.

according to the biblical-theological metanarrative that discloses a grace-filled metaphysic and a generative morality.

Nietzsche wrote about a myriad of topics, yet there are repetitive themes in most of his works, including theology, identity, meaning, morality, truth, faith, and hope. Building from the hermeneutical boundaries outlined in this introduction, I will entertain these topics from within the biblical-theological narrative. Working from within the biblical storyline in Part 2, I will attempt to critique and out-narrate Nietzsche in each of the aforementioned themes. As will be shown in chapter 1, Nietzsche understood his critical method as more than a descriptive evaluation of cultural ideologies; he was attempting to debunk and dethrone such cultural and religious ideologies to disclose a better way. My aim in each chapter is to turn Nietzsche upside down to illustrate that he *often* parodies the biblical narrative. Part 2 serves as a biblical and theological grounding for the cultural conversations in Part 3, which attempts to generate some practical implications for a public theology in a Nietzschean age. Part 3 invites the church to convictionally and confessionally critique and out-narrate culture's own Nietzschean-inspired ideologies and philosophies.

Concerning methodology and aims, this project draws from the deep recesses of Augustine, especially his *City of God*. In that work, Augustine "reads" Roman culture through the lens of Scripture and the Christian imagination. Likewise, I will attempt to reveal our own cultural gods and ideologies through the lens of Scripture and the Christian theological imagination.

Part Two

Parodies

A parody is creative work that both playfully imitates and mocks other works for comedic effect. Yet, such comedy is not for mere entertainment purposes. Parodies persuade at an emotional register, competing for the audience's affections so that they might see the world differently. Parody exaggerates original works for critical purposes. Nietzsche's writings in the 1880s were largely parodical, especially *Ecce Homo*. For Nietzsche, the rhetorical styles of ancient Greek philosophy and medieval Christian scholasticism were too dry, logic-centered, impractical, outdated, and unscientific. Instead, he largely uses parody and satire to mock Greco-Christian traditions to persuade his readers of a better way and a new future *without* those traditions. As noted in the introduction, Nietzsche viewed his work as a dismantling of cultural and religious ideologies, and I will argue in the next several chapters that his own writings often mirror and, in many cases, parody biblical narratives. Ironically though, I wish to show that Scripture always already out-narrates and critiques Nietzschean notions of theology (chapter 2), identity (chapter 3), meaning and morality (chapter 4), and truth (chapter 5).

Chapter 1

Inviting Nietzsche to Church

After discussing Friedrich Nietzsche for a few weeks with students in my Introduction to Philosophy class nearly a decade ago, I asked them, "What if Nietzsche was right? Or what if Nietzsche was even partly correct? How would it change the way you lived in and experienced the world?" After a long pause, I told them, "I've tricked you. Sadly, you're thinking of those questions as hypotheticals, as *what ifs*, and not as actuals. Nietzsche *has* changed how we think about, view, and live in our daily world." Already by 1910 (only a decade after Nietzsche's death), an American writer documented, "Friedrich Nietzsche has begun to invade this country. . . . The slow but persistent growth of [his] fame is one of the intellectual romances of our time."[1] My point was this: While Nietzsche may be physically dead, he's nevertheless alive and well in Western culture and continues to exert enormous authority in our daily lives.

---

[1] Jennifer Ratner-Rosenhagen, *American Nietzsche: A History of an Icon and His Ideas* (University of Chicago Press, 2012), 68.

I acknowledge that philosophy is not always an easy subject; it requires an enormous amount of wrestling, doubt, confusion, humility, and hope. From the Presocratics to the Poststructuralists, I still read many of their works and leave more confused than when I started them. And even though Nietzsche has highly and intentionally ambiguous claims and concepts in his writings, I return to him year after year. Here is the main reason why an evangelical, Baptist Christian like myself reads an Enlightenment, positivist, atheist philosopher: Even though most Americans have never read a single page of Nietzsche, they are indebted to him—as the questions to my college students highlight. One primary objective of this book is to excavate Nietzsche's philosophical proposal while exposing those thoughts and themes found in American cultural philosophies and practices.[2]

To attain this task of introducing this German giant, this chapter is structured into two parts: the first being genealogical

---

[2] I am not suggesting that Nietzsche's themes are perfectly reappropriated into our cultural moment. Any person who suggests such a move is blind to historical, cultural, social, philosophical, and economic developments of the past 125 years since Nietzsche's death. Rather, it is historically and methodologically safer to conclude that there are *appropriations* of Nietzsche that we must be attentive to—not a singular appropriation but plural appropriation*s*. We might even refer to them as Nietzscheanisms where persons, groups, organizations, and societies have highlighted specific teachings of Nietzsche and reappropriated them for their specific contexts. Yet, we can safely conclude that a common thread is woven through each of these Nietzscheanisms: "But what almost all [Nietzscheans] had in common was a general desire to challenge and go beyond accepted assumptions and conventions." Steven E. Aschheim, *The Nietzsche Legacy in Germany 1890–1990* (University of California Press, 1992), 310. We will examine some of these cultural Nietzscheanisms of America throughout this work.

in its orientation and the second methodological. In the first section, I will introduce relevant biographical chapters of Nietzsche's thought, method, philosophical arc, and conclusions about the Western metanarrative with particular attention to **metaphysics** and **morality**.[3] As will become evident, Nietzsche not only expected the rise of a new era of human history, but he also elicited one too. In some of his writings like *Thus Spoke Zarathustra*, Nietzsche even envisions himself as a prophetic character in a transitional age where the old is passing away and a new age is dawning.[4]

The second part of this chapter Nietzsche would find repulsive because of its simplicity and its focus on systematization—both anathema for Nietzsche because he prized philosophical complexity.[5] But for the sake of clarity and space, this latter section is intentionally structured to engage with Nietzsche's framework from *within* a biblical-theological framework—at this point, Nietzsche is probably rolling over in his grave.[6] In this

---

[3] Meant to be a helpful tool for the reader, all **emboldened** terms are defined and further clarified in the Glossary at the end of this book.

[4] Not only is "dawn" a ubiquitous metaphor in Nietzsche's works, but it's also the title of his 1881 publication *Daybreak*, which could also be translated from German as *The Dawn of Day*.

[5] See Bruce Ellis Benson, *Graven Ideologies: Nietzsche, Derrida, and Marion on Modern Idolatry* (IVP Academic, 2002), ch. 1; Gilles Deleuze, *Nietzsche and Philosophy*, trans. Hugh Tomlinson (Columbia University Press, 1983), 3–6.

[6] In chapter 1, I will elucidate Nietzsche's disgust of particular metanarratives, especially the Christian one. The fact that I will read him from *within* a biblical-theological metanarrative would have erupted outrage from Nietzsche, because his highest aim was to unhinge Western society from Christianity's inabilities to provide true "redemption." Christianity, he might say, offers an illusory hope because it's an otherworldly, intangible promise always beyond our reach.

latter section, I will also sketch the methodological boundaries of my work. In short, I want to survey a (methodological) topography of how I expect to interact with Nietzsche and his philosophical project. To use Reinhold Niebuhr's famous frameworks, there are three overarching cultural methods or approaches for Christians to consider: Christ *against* culture, Christ *of* culture, and Christ *above* culture.[7] In respective order, the first underscores an opposition between Christ and culture, the second emphasizes agreements between the two, and the last model illustrates the primacy and otherness of Christianity. Later, I will provide a methodological survey of how I will interact with Nietzsche's philosophical project. Using Reinhold Niebuhr's famous cultural typology as a point of departure, I will frame Nietzsche's work as a cultural parody of Christianity.

The Intellectual Topography of Nineteenth-Century Germany

During my PhD studies, we were required to take and pass two theological language classes. Unless you had a particular field of study, most students took the default classes: German and French. Of all languages that could be learned, why German and French? It's because they are considered the "academic languages" of the last three centuries. In other words, Germany and France were the academic ivory towers that held significant influence not only in Europe but globally, and knowledge of these languages enables one to study dozens of key historical figures.

---

[7] Reinhold Niehbur, *Christ and Culture* (Harper & Row, 1975).

Germany in the eighteenth and nineteenth centuries was an intellectual *tour de force*. A brief glance at history would unfold Germany's impact in the areas of art (Wilhelm von Kobell and Joseph Anton Koch) science (Karl Müller), mathematics (Carl Friedrich Gauss), astronomy (William Herschel), music (Felix Mendelssohn, Johann Sebastian Bach, Richard Wagner), and especially philosophy and theology. These last two subjects in particular are especially pertinent for our understanding of Nietzsche's intellectual environment and require a brief survey.

Nietzsche was a brilliant man, who was well-read across various fields of study. In Nietzsche's own backyard, notable historical-critical methods of biblical interpretation (text criticism, literary criticism, and form criticism) were exploding, and key biblical scholars and theologians like Julius Wellhausen, Hermann Gunkel, and David Strauss were Nietzsche's intellectual contemporaries. Describing the historical-critical methods developed by these German thinkers, Wolfgang Rolf writes:

> The different disciplines of the historical-critical method contribute to the understanding of a given passage, i.e. *textual criticism* tries to determine the text as it left the author's hands, *literary criticism* discusses the import of idiom, form, and historical background of the passage, *form criticism* attempts to determine the original life situation of the oral (or literary) pattern used, *semantic studies* trace the etymology of a given word within the family of languages to which the language of the text belongs and describe the history of that word, that is the changes in meaning and usage it underwent. To these aspects of the historical-critical method has now to be

> added *tradition criticism* which attempts a reconstruction of the impact a passage was designed to exercise and of the impacts it actually made during its transmission during the Biblical periods.[8]

Because these historical-critical methods were producing novel and surprising results, they became the sensational hermeneutical methods for biblical scholars at European and American universities to both mimic and master. For instance, the Old Testament scholar Hermann Gunkel wrote *The Legends of Genesis* partially as a commentary on Genesis, but Gunkel's primary aim was to demonstrate the oral and textual layers behind (or between) the scenes in the composition of Genesis. He refers to such oral collectors of these traditions as the Jahvist (Yahwist), Elohist, and Priestly sources. He writes:

> The collection of the legends in writing was not done by one hand or at one period, but in the course of a very long process by several or many hands. We distinguish two stages in this process: the older, to which we owe the collections of the Jahvist designated by 'J' and the Elohist designated by 'E,' and then a later, thorough revision in what is known as the Priestly Codex 'P.'[9]

Gunkel's proposal is that in Genesis and other biblical literature, orality preceded their literary and creative construction, and

---

[8] Wolfgang M. W. Rolf, "The Historical-Critical Method and Its Function in Biblical Interpretation," *Indian Journal of Theology* 12 (1963): 51–58. All emphases are mine to highlight the different types of historical-critical methods.

[9] Hermann Gunkel, *The Legends of Genesis*, trans. W. H. Curruth (Open Court, 1901), 124.

the aim of serious scholarship should be to excavate those oral and literary threads to better understand how and why the Bible was constructed.

The impact of these novel forms of biblical scholarship on Nietzsche can be detected in a letter he wrote to his friend Paul Deussen, where Nietzsche confessed, "What undermined [Christianity], without our noticing, was the superb historical-critical method which we employed, in Pforta, to torment the ancients and which then, quite by itself, applied itself to biblical matters."[10] Pforta was a prestigious boarding school in Germany that Nietzsche attended from 1858–1864. Shortly after leaving Pforta for theological studies in Bonn, Nietzsche consumed Protestant theologian David Strauss's *Life of Jesus*, a work where Strauss used historical-critical methods to reassess the New Testament Gospels' accounts of Jesus. Strauss's thesis was that the Gospels represent mythological accounts of the historical Jesus, who never actually performed any miracles. The role of the historian, then, is to "peel back" the mythical layers to get at the real historical husk. Working through numerous fragments of Nietzsche's writings on religious themes in his early studies at Bonn, philosopher Julian Young notes how Nietzsche's "thinking was influenced by Strauss. Although produced by a theology student, the standpoint of these fragments is that, not that of a believer, but of an external, indeed hostile, observer."[11] These theological ruminations in the mid-1860s germinated into Nietzsche's more mature critiques of Christianity that would come in the next two decades.

---

[10] Quoted in Julian Young, *Friedrich Nietzsche: A Philosophical Biography* (Cambridge University Press, 2010), 29.

[11] Young, *Friedrich Nietzsche*, 57.

Undoubtedly, the rise of historical-critical methods, exemplified in Gunkel and Strauss, had enormous impact on the traditions and redactory threads within biblical literature. Yet, in the process of exploring these methods, German scholarship introduced a particular academic *Zeitgeist* into biblical studies, which comprised three features: (1) the Bible is *only* a human construction; (2) the Bible must be deconstructed, or that is, mastered; and (3) the Bible is to be demythologized. Again, these characteristics were so ingrained into the *ethos* of German academia that they continued to haunt German scholarship for another half century, as evident in the work of the early twentieth-century New Testament scholar Rudolf Bultmann.[12]

Another well-respected German theologian, whom Nietzsche adored, was Ludwig Feuerbach, who established a psychological hermeneutic where God was an anthropological projection of our deepest fears. In Feuerbach's words, "Religion is the disuniting of man from himself; he sets God before him as the antithesis of himself."[13] According to Feuerbach, it is in and through this disuniting of a person from himself that a psychic abstracting and absolutizing of himself may occur: "Only by and in the understanding has man the power of abstraction from

---

[12] One of Bultmann's most notable works is *The New Testament and Mythology and Other Basic Writings*, ed. and trans. S. M. Ogden (Fortress, 1984) where Bultmann asks, "Can Christian preaching expect modern man *to accept the mythical view of the world as true?* To do so would be both senseless and impossible" (3). The three characteristics above are so inherent in Bultmann's question that they are the epistemic default: To think, consider, and imagine otherwise is to be unscientific and foolish. Unsurprisingly, this epistemic default continues to saturate Western imaginations from academia to rural America.

[13] Ludwig Feuerbach, *The Essence of Christianity*, trans. Marian Evans (Cambridge University Press, 2012), 31.

himself, from his subjective being—of exalting himself to general ideas and relations, of distinguishing the object from the impressions which it produces on his feelings."[14] When the religious person performs this projective act, he disempowers himself and thereby empowers a fiction of his imagination. For Feuerbach, we need to rediscover and harness our inner psychic strength, not give it away to an idol-like illusion.[15]

In summary, the demythologizing and the psychologizing of the Bible were authoritative and domineering virtues in the social imaginary of German academia. Even if Nietzsche was not personally acquainted with all the European scholars mentioned above, the academic spirit that transcended their scholarship held conceptual, intellectual, and existential gravitas for Nietzsche. "We stand," Nietzsche submits regarding his intellectual environment, "at the threshold of a great revolution when the mass of mankind first grasps that the whole fabric of Christianity rests on [mere] assumptions: the existence of God, immortality, the authority of the Bible will always remain problematic."[16] In short, the Christian faith lacked any serious plausibility structure for most of European culture during this period, and Nietzsche wanted to deconstruct Western metaphysics and morality in order to inaugurate a revolutionary age beyond the Greco-Christian worldview.[17]

---

[14] Feuerbach, *Essence of Christianity*, 32.

[15] Feuerbach, *Essence of Christianity*, 27.

[16] Young, *Friedrich Nietzsche*, 35.

[17] "Plausibility structure" was coined and described by sociologist Peter Berger in his book, *The Sacred Canopy* (Doubleday, 1967). Even though originally a sociological term, many theologians and philosophers have adopted it to mean the *social legitimacy* of a worldview in a particular culture. In the case of our present discussion, the Christian world view became untenable and illegitimate in nineteenth-century Germany.

Nietzsche and the Seeds of Critical Theory

Not only was Nietzsche a powerful poet, a musical critic, an artist, a classically trained philologist, and an erudite philosopher, he was foremost a critical theorist. To put it simply, social and critical theories engage with "complex determinations between power, ideology, and economic forces in constituting social life."[18] An underlying assumption of many critical theories is that all social life is anthropologically constructed or "man-made." However, if policies, programs, and politics are man-made, then these two questions must be asked: First, who made them? And, more importantly, who in power constructed them? If critical theorists can trace the genealogy of power, then they can pinpoint the origins of the powers, ideologies, and forces embedded within the contours of our social lives. In his introduction to critical theory, Stephen Bronner writes, "Deeply skeptical of tradition and all absolute claims, critical theory was always concerned not merely with how things were but how they might be and should be."[19] But locating these powers is only part of the critical theorist's project; they want to expose the powers that be to expunge them. The twofold aim of most critical theories is destruction and construction; they destroy the traditional to chart and erect the revolutionary.

Throughout this work, we will emphasize the critical theory within and underneath the writings of Nietzsche. He was deeply

---

[18] Watkin, *Biblical Critical Theory*, 28. In Part 2, I will not only utilize Watkin's understanding of critique, but I will also implement his biblical-theological method to converse with Nietzsche's philosophy.

[19] Stephen Eric Bronner, *Critical Theory: A Very Short Introduction* (Oxford University Press, 2011), 1.

concerned with the powers that dominated Western society (read: Christianity), and he hoped to expose them as *the* domineering power of all social life, from politics to economics, social relations to metaphysics, morality to truth and faith. In short, Nietzsche holds that these Greco-Christian ideologies must be disrobed to reveal their true selves—weak, feeble, and inhumane oppressors who have fabricated a sophisticated set of ideologies that we are all enslaved to.

In response to these deeply embedded cultural ideologies, Nietzsche unleashes his genealogical method.[20] Simply stated, a genealogical reading is a form of critique intended to overturn culturally accepted norms to reveal their true values and origins. Gilles Deleuze describes critical philosophies like Nietzsche's genealogy as "the referring back of all things and any kind of origin to values, but also the referring back of these values to something which is, as it were, their origin and determines their value."[21] To get a feel for this genealogical method, we will briefly explore two of Nietzsche's major works—*Twilight of the Idols* and *On the Genealogy of Morals*—where his genealogical method exposes the origins and values of ancient Greek and Christian thought.

---

[20] Deleuze comments on the nature of Nietzsche's philosophy: "This is Nietzsche's twofold struggle: against those who remove values from criticism, contenting themselves with producing inventories of existing values or with criticising things in the name of established values; but also against those who criticize, or respect, values by deriving them from simple facts, from so-called 'objective facts'" (*Nietzsche and Philosophy*, 2). We will deal more with the topics of morality and meaning in chapter 3, where we discuss Nietzsche's longing for a "transvaluation of values."

[21] Deleuze, *Nietzsche and Philosophy*, 2.

In *Twilight of the Idols*, Nietzsche introduces his weapon of choice to sound out all idols: the philosophical hammer. "Here for once to ask questions with a *hammer* and, perhaps, to hear in response that famous hollow sound which speaks of swollen innards."[22] As Bruce Ellis Benson illustrates, "It might be thought that the hammer here is a literal hammer for smashing idols to bits. . . . Yet his 'hammer' is much more subtle. It is a tuning hammer, used to check whether our so-called realities ring true, or whether they have a 'hollow sound' demonstrating that they are mere idols."[23] Such a subtle tap on so-called realities, or in Nietzsche's language "eternal idols," will reveal what or, better, *whose* they are.

An eternal idol is a conceptual reference to any narrative or worldview that underscores a life beyond this one, such as certain ancient Greek and Christian traditions of an afterlife. In his biography of Nietzsche, Julian Young captures the German's aversion to the eternal idol of Christianity: "It seems to me possible that one of the things the mature Nietzsche held, at least unconsciously, against the Christian worldview was that, with its reduction of this world to a cold and draughty waiting-room we sinners are forced to inhabit prior to our departure for the 'true' world above."[24] For Nietzsche, these eternalized idols and ideologies invoke our allegiance and attention,[25] and we worship them with unwavering devotion and evangelize

---

[22] Nietzsche, *Twilight of the Idols: How to Philosophize with a Hammer*, trans. Duncan Large (Oxford University Press, 1998), 3.

[23] Benson, *Graven Ideologies*, 40.

[24] Young, *Friedrich Nietzsche*, 11.

[25] See Benson's introduction in *Graven Ideologies* where he connects the terms "idol," "idea," and "ideology" in Nietzschean thought.

about their truthfulness and reality.[26] Benson, highlighting Nietzsche's concern, states, "Ideology suggests a skewed conception of reality. . . . And if ideologies are held dogmatically, idols are often held even more so. So they are our creations (and since we like the look of ourselves), we are hard pressed to give them up."[27] For Nietzsche, then, the issue is largely epistemological and existential. From his perspective, most of the European society of his day had been fed a faulty perspective, a system that told them these eternal things *are* true orientations to reality, but in the end they are hollow representations that fail to generate life. This is where Nietzsche explicitly borrows from Feuerbach.

As alluded to earlier in this introduction, for Nietzsche eternal idols (*à la* Feuerbachian religious psychology) are absolutized ideas a society devotes its life to defending and promoting. Once the hammer taps on these eternal ideas, hollowness rings back, demonstrating their true values and origins. Commenting on Nietzsche's philosophical move, Alasdair MacIntyre states, "Nietzsche's invitation to such an agent is first to investigate the genealogy of her present normative and evaluative judgments and then to recognize, in light of that genealogy, the discreditable nature of the hold that they have upon her."[28] Metaphysics, according to Nietzsche, is not a reality beyond our existence

[26] Speaking about devotion to ideologies, Nietzsche writes, "They [Greek and Christian philosophers] kill things and stuff them, these servants of conceptual idols, when they worship—they become a mortal danger to everything when they worship" (*Twilight of the Idols*, 16).

[27] Benson, *Graven Ideologies*, 24.

[28] Alasdair MacIntyre, *Ethics in the Conflicts of Modernity: An Essay on Desire, Practical Reasoning, and Narrative* (Cambridge University Press, 2016), 42.

(hence, *meta*physics) but merely absolutized ideas. Once the philosophical hammer is used, we discover metaphysics to be nothing more than a societal and "man-made" slant that was internalized and accepted as true.[29] Nietzsche's hope is to fully demythologize and psychologize metaphysics and morality. In short, these two schemas of metaphysics and morality are immanentized, and when we are confronted with a conventional narrative or norm, we must, says Nietzsche, see it as a symptom with a causal, historical force.

Nietzsche's hope is to fully demythologize and psychologize metaphysics and morality.

On Method: Nietzschean Parodies and Christianity's Promises

In the previous sections of this introductory chapter, we briefly outlined some of the German intellectual influences upon Nietzsche while emphasizing some of his philosophical thrusts, most notably, the exposing and dismantling of powers to commence a grand revolution. As promised, this second part of the chapter will erect the practical methodology embraced by this project. Rather than just delivering a historical reading of

---

[29] Nietzsche's thoughts here on European society's reception of Christian ideas and ideologies is what later critical theorists refer to as "internal oppression." An internal oppression is a socialized way of "thinking that justified the status quo, making it seem right, just, fair, desirable, natural, and inevitable." See Neil Shenvi and Pat Sawyer, *Critical Dilemma: The Rise of Critical Theories and Social Justice Ideology: Implications for the Church and Society* (Harvest House, 2023), 118.

Nietzsche, I want this book to posit some creative ways to interact with and go beyond Nietzsche. So, as I see it, it is imperative to demonstrate how I will interact with Nietzsche from this point forward.

Carl Trueman in his most recent work on critical theory, *To Change All Worlds*, develops a helpful model for us: "The challenge to which critical theory therefore summons the church is to show, not merely to argue, that she has the answers. Critical theory does not so much provide Christians with a useful tool to think about the world as clarify a set of questions to which we have the answers already, if only we open our eyes to see them."[30] Trueman's last sentence offers both the approach and goal of this current project. We might even say that it offers conceptual parameters and a lexical landscape for *The Devil Reads Nietzsche.* This book neither "baptizes" Nietzsche nor "plunders" Nietzschean concepts, language, or methods. Even though he is interacting specifically with a wide array of critical theories, Trueman's wisdom is relevant for the present task. First, this book will illustrate how and why Nietzsche raised certain challenges to Christianity, and second, it will demonstrate how Christianity *already* has answers to those Nietzschean challenges. We might say, then, that my intentions are neither very extravagant nor extraordinary; they are rather modest in scope. I shall argue that the biblical narrative always already answers the questions and challenges Nietzsche raised and proposed. Nietzsche insists that a philosophical revolution will inaugurate a new humanity and new society, and the way forward is to put to death the old society with its deathly metanarratives and terminal metaphysics.

---

[30] Carl Trueman, *To Change All Worlds: Critical Theory from Marx to Marcuse* (B&H Academic, 2024), 227.

Ironically, as we shall see, in describing this philosophical revolution Nietzsche actually borrows from a Christian narrative soaked with stories about slavery and freedom, oppression and hope, and death and resurrection.

We might call Nietzsche's philosophical mission a "parody" or an exaggerated imitation of the Christian story, and this brings us full circle to the promise made earlier referencing Reinhold Niebuhr. To reiterate, I briefly recalled Niebuhr's three methodological approaches: Christ *against* culture, Christ *of* culture, and Christ *above* culture. I hinted at a fourth option, which is this: Culture *parodies* Christianity. Now, you may suspect a hint of Niebuhr's "Christ above culture" in this phrase, yet as I already noted, this fourth option would be distinct and yet adjacent to one of Niebuhr's categories.

> Nietzsche insists that a philosophical revolution will inaugurate a new humanity and new society, and the way forward is to put to death the old society with its deathly metanarratives and terminal metaphysics.

To claim that culture parodies Christianity is to affirm the primacy of the Christian narrative and the proclamation that "there is another king—Jesus" (Acts 17:7). Seemingly sovereign lords, kings, emperors, policies, and philosophies are servants and subordinates to the true king, whose kingdom reigns. Second, such a paradigm underscores the preexistence of the Christian faith within cultural and philosophical interactions. As Trueman noted above, cultural philosophies like Nietzsche's are not "useful tools" with which Christians might think about the world. Rather, according to the paradigm I am proposing, the Christian narrative is prioritized, whereby it interprets cultural teachings and philosophies as misdirected and misoriented because they are deviations, or parodies, of the Christian faith.

Here I am intentionally drawing from John Milbank's approach in *Theology and Social Theory*, where he argues that modernity's (and postmodernity's) teachings are modifications or rejections of orthodox Christianity.[31] Following Milbank, here is my bold methodological claim: Modern Western cultural philosophies are distortions and parodies of orthodox Christianity. Within the theology and philosophical veins of Milbank, my purpose is not to contrast Nietzsche with Christianity. Such an approach is all too common among modern authors, whereby two positions are placed side by side, and arguments are weighed by the reader—acting as a juror—to make a choice between the two differing accounts. Instead of requesting a "guilty" or "not guilty" verdict, readers and hearers are summoned to answer "true" or "false."

Allow me to elaborate further. Milbank writes that modern philosophies like Nietzsche's project are "*mythos*, and therefore cannot be refuted, but only out-narrated, if we can persuade people—for reasons of 'literary taste'—that Christianity offers a much better story."[32] Commenting on Milbank's methodology, James K. A. Smith adds that this approach points "to the mythical status of competing ontologies and narratives and offers a counter-narrative from the Christian story that is embodied in practice."[33] To be abundantly clear, my methodological pur-

---

[31] Milbank, *Theology and Social Theory*, 1.

[32] Milbank, *Theology and Social Theory*, 330.

[33] James K. A. Smith, *Introducing Radical Orthodoxy: Mapping a Post-Secular Theology* (Baker Academic, 2004), 180.

pose is, first, to carefully read Nietzsche and, second, to allow the Christian narrative to out-narrate the German philosopher. I plan to fulfill this overarching purpose by locating the internal antinomies and inconsistencies within Nietzsche. In other words, I want you to wade into the undercurrents of Nietzsche's philosophy with me in order to experience the fractures, tensions, and implications of Nietzschean thinking for a person's life.[34]

When you reach the end of this book, you should be better equipped with a theological imagination that *out-narrates* Nietzsche and several contemporary philosophies that have been birthed from his writings. As Chris Watkin positively captures, "Out-narrating is not about telling the better story in the sense of being the most gripping or necessarily satisfying; it is about telling the bigger story, the story within which all other stories find their place."[35] Nietzsche desired to lead European society toward cultural renewal by inviting a developing culture into a better story. As much as he wanted to demythologize Christianity and the Christianized worldview, his philosophical quest was not anti-theological but deeply theological (more on this in chapter 2).

---

[34] You may hear echoes of Francis Schaeffer's apologetical approach known as "taking the roof off." A roof provides protection from the weathers of life, and once it's removed, Schaeffer notes that "each man must stand naked and wounded before the truth of what is." Schaeffer adds, "The truth that we let in first is not a dogmatic statement of the truth of the Scriptures, but the truth of the external world and the truth of what man himself is. This is what shows him his need. The Scriptures then show him the real nature of his lostness and the answer to it." See Schaeffer, *A Christian View of Philosophy and Culture*, vol. 1 of *The Complete Works of Francis A. Schaeffer: A Christian Worldview* (Crossway, 1994), 133–35, 138, and 140–41. We will directly engage with Schaeffer's method in the last chapter.

[35] Watkin, *Biblical Critical Theory*, 21.

Attempting to destroy conceptual idols, he established new ones; attempting to destroy metaphysics, he erected a new one; attempting to bury Christian morality, he birthed new ones. For Nietzsche and even modern-day critical theorists, their intellectual quests are quasi-religious, because they "give an account of our brokenness, an explanation of the reasons for pain, a saving story accompanied by strong ethical imperatives, and hope for the future."[36]

> Nietzsche desired to lead European society toward cultural renewal by inviting a developing culture into a better story.

As will be shown in the following chapters, Nietzsche borrows or, better yet, plagiarizes the Christian narrative to develop his own *mythos*, a post-Enlightenment, post-Christian narrative with new gods (Dionysius), a new humanity (a human *becoming*), a new metaphysic (a spiritualized immanence), a new fall (which he calls *décadence*), a new set of prophetic proclamations (whom he calls Zarathustra), and a salvation inaugurated by a messianic figure (the *Übermensch*). Nietzsche wants to inaugurate a new society and humanity without the taints of Christianity, yet, curiously, he steals the narratival structure and lexicon of the biblical canon (creation-fall-redemption-new creation) to elicit and erect this future realm. In order to locate the parodies within Nietzschean thinking, I will address two questions in each chapter: What are the central inconsistencies and tensions within Nietzsche's writings, and what are their existential implications?

---

[36] Elizabeth C. Corey, "First Church of Intersectionality," *First Things*, August 2017, https://www.firstthings.com/article/2017/08/first-church-of-intersectionality.

Chapter 2

In the Beginning, God Is Dead (On Theology)

Nietzsche's name in our time has been indelibly linked with four ideas, the death of God, nihilism, the will to power, and the *Übermensch*."[1] Michael Allen Gillespie here rightly characterizes what ideas made Nietzsche famous in the Western world. Yet, *how* he became famous is a key feature in need of further exploration. Christians typically have knee-jerk reactions when they hear Nietzsche's singular phrase "God is dead," and from experience they usually misunderstand and thereby mischaracterize what Nietzsche meant. As noted in the introductory chapter, certain parts of Nietzsche's teachings have been received and (re)appropriated by a diverse collection of persons, groups, and societies for over a century. The dual aim of this current project is to both sensitively attend to Nietzsche's philosophical

[1] Michael Allen Gillespie, *Nietzsche's Final Teaching* (University of Chicago Press, 2017), 41.

project while carefully considering those various modern cultural and social appropriations.

As a reminder, this project is not a comprehensive study of Nietzsche. Rather, it *introduces* his more infamous works and iconic themes. Rather than focusing on the development of Nietzsche's theology throughout his corpus, I will choose his latter works to highlight his theology.[2] My ambition in this chapter is to first explicate a Nietzschean theology and then put him in conversation with the alternative theological vision of Genesis 1–3. As we will see, understanding Nietzsche can give us invaluable insights into our present cultural philosophies. Nietzsche was a titanic impetus for how we have come to imagine (or not imagine) God today.

Understanding Nietzsche can give us invaluable insights into our present cultural philosophies.

The Origins of God and the Rise and Fall of Metaphysics

Nietzsche had a grand vision for Western society that orbited around the question, "How can society be nudged into a new

[2] One of my former professors often quipped, "Last words are lasting words." Even though he was referencing Jesus's last words on the cross, the maxim is also fitting for our topic. Nietzsche's lasting influence—philosophical and theological—is largely due to the writings published in the final six years of his career, which include *The Gay Science* (1882), *Thus Spoke Zarathustra* (1883–1885), *Beyond Good and Evil* (1886), *On the Genealogy of Morals* (1887), *The Twilight of Idols* (1888), *The Anti-Christ* (1888), and *Ecce Homo* (1888).

metaphysic and morality?"[3] Due to the Jewish, Christian, and ancient Greek historical narratives, Nietzsche contended that European society had been in theological, metaphysical, and metanarratival shackles, and within the spirit of the Enlightenment project, he offered philosophical deliverance from such institutional bondages. Generally speaking, many European Enlightenment figures perceived themselves as living at a historical tipping point. Not only did this modern experience evoke scientific and technological advances, but it also birthed enormous developments in industrialization, urbanization, globalization, and ethics—including novel forms of expressive individualism and instrumental rationality.[4]

Building on this Enlightenment spirit of progress, Nietzsche read history as evolving beyond where it had been, especially relating to conversations surrounding theology. For him, there are several interconnected origin(s) of God. First, Enlightenment society was erected on an omnipresent idea or ideology inherited from a Christianized society ("Christendom"), thus making most of the global population influenced by a socioreligious power. We might call this the *democratic thesis* because people in power abuse their social status to sway others into their values, cultures, ways,

[3] Terms associated with this pursuit include the "transvaluation of values."

[4] For more on this historical tipping point in the Enlightenment, see Alasdair MacIntyre, "Science, Stories, and Our Knowledge of the Natural World," in *All Things Hold Together in Christ: A Conversation on Faith, Science, and Virtue*, ed. James K. A. Smith and Michael L. Gulker (Baker Academic, 2018), 339–56. See also Alister McGrath, *Scientific Theology: Theory* (T&T Clark, 2006); and Adam B. Seligman, *Modernity's Wager: Authority, the Self, and Transcendence* (Princeton University Press, 2000).

rules, ideas, and politics. Second, the majority in Christendom self-authorize their cultural power along with their preferred stories, metaphors, and ideas to establish societal norms, ideologies, and practices. We will call this the *demagogue thesis* due to its intentional manufacturing of ideas and practices to excite the masses into buying into particular ideologies. Third, Nietzsche holds that those in positions of authority in Christendom standardize teachings on God, metaphysics, the supernatural, and morality as means of gaining social power. In this manner, God is invoked as an omnipresent idea for power consolidation rather than a real, personal, omnipotent being. We'll call this the *deification thesis*. Nietzsche narrates this historical process in both his *On the Genealogy of Morals* and *Ecce Homo*. In the foreword of *Ecce Homo*, Nietzsche writes:

> The "real world" and the "apparent world"—in plain words: the *fake* world and reality . . . The *lie* of the ideal has till now been the curse on reality; on its account humanity itself has become fake and false right down to its deepest instincts—to the point of worshipping values *opposite* to the only ones which would guarantee it a flourishing, a future, the exalted *right* to a future.[5]

In Nietzsche's larger corpus, the "real world" is the hermeneutical slant or spin contrived by a majority. The real world is not *really* real; it is a perspective of the world so entrenched in a society that it *seems to be* obvious and true. In *Twilight of the Idols*, Nietzsche creatively narrates how this "real world" is, at best, a fable:

---

[5] Nietzsche, *Ecce Homo: How to Become What You Are*, trans. Duncan Large (Oxford University Press, 2009), 3.

HOW THE 'REAL WORLD' FINALLY BECAME A FABLE

History of an Error

1. The real world attainable for the wise man, the pious man, the virtuous man—he lives in it, he is it.
   (Most ancient form of the idea, relatively clever, simple, convincing. Paraphrase of the proposition: 'I, Plato, am the truth').
2. The real world unattainable for now, but promised to the wise man, the pious man, the virtuous man ('to the sinner who repents'). (Progress of the idea: it becomes more cunning, more insidious, more incomprehensible—it becomes a woman, it becomes Christian—)
3. The real world unattainable, unprovable, unpromisable, but the mere thought of it a consolation, an obligation, an imperative. (The old sun in the background, but seen through mist and scepticism; the idea become sublime, pale, Nordic, Königsbergian.)
4. The real world—unattainable? At any rate unattained. And since unattained also unknown. Hence no consolation, redemption, obligation either: what could something unknown oblige us to do? (Break of day. First yawn of reason. Cock-crow of positivism.)
5. The 'real world'—an idea with no further use, no longer even an obligation—an idea become useless, superfluous, therefore a refuted idea: let us do away with it! (Broad daylight; breakfast; return of *bons sens* and cheerfulness; Plato's shameful blush; din from all free spirits.)

6. The real world—we have done away with it: what world was left? the apparent one, perhaps?—But no! with the real world we have also done away with the apparent one! (Noon; moment of the shortest shadow; end of the longest error; pinnacle of humanity; *INCIPIT ZARATHUSTRA.*)[6]

This work poetically crafts a genealogical narrative of Western society from its beginnings to its diminishing death.[7] As can be seen, Nietzsche generates a peculiar myth, a particular telling of history. We could say then that Nietzsche is mythologizing or at least *re*mythologizing history (more on myth in chapter 5).

Allow me to offer some commentary to his chapter cited above. Reaching back to Plato as the originator of the "real world" (Western metaphysics), Nietzsche suggests this philosopher inaugurated the "history of error." Each of the six paragraphs of this chapter function like times of a day—from moments before twilight to noon—and each of these times are symbolic of epochs within Western history. They begin with the phrase, "The real world," and then Nietzsche delivers a descriptive label for how each epoch understood its own metaphysical claims:

---

[6] Nietzsche, *Twilight of the Idols: How to Philosophize with a Hammer*, trans. Duncan Large (Oxford University Press, 2008), 20.

[7] Nietzsche crafted this chapter with fine detail because he believed that art should inform philosophy.

EPOCHAL AGE	NAME OF EPOCH	DESCRIPTION OF EPOCH
Epoch 1	Socratic	Its "real world" is "attainable" through wisdom, piety, and virtue. This metaphysics is transcendent yet immanent, or as Nietzsche states, "he lives in it, *he is it.*"
Epoch 2	Christian	Its "real world" is "unattainable for now," but promised by God for the wise, pious, and virtuous who repents. Nietzsche also begins to narrate movement in time here because there is "Progress of the idea." When character is formed by virtue, one can see truth rightly but not attain it until later (i.e., heaven).
Epoch 3	Kantian/ Königsbergian (Kant lived most of his life in Königberg.)	Its "real world" is questionably "unattainable," "unprovable," and "unpromisable" because of the epistemological gap between immanence and transcendence. Time continues to move forward in history as "the sun [is] in the background, but seen through mist." In short, metaphysics becomes foggy and difficult to ascertain.

Epoch 4	Positivist/ Auguste Comte	Its “real world” is questionably “unattainable” making it completely “unknown.” This, for Nietzsche, begins a “Break of day,” a “First yawn of reason,” a “Cock-crow” for an awakening metaphysics. Nietzsche’s poetic paradox cannot be overlooked, because it is in this historical epoch of Comte that through metaphysics’ awakening, it’s actually dying.
Epoch 5	Schopenhauerian	The “real world” is an “idea of no further use, no longer even an obligation.” This is the time of “Broad daylight,” where all of life can be seen clearly, and not only clearly, but this time offers liberty (“free spirits”).
Epoch 6	Nietzschean	“The real world” has “been done away with” because Nietzsche’s prophetic character Zarathustra has spoken at “Noon,” the “moment of the shortest shadow,” the “end of the longest error [of metaphysics],” and the rise and “pinnacle of humanity.”

Nietzsche is retelling the story of Western history, yet he enriches it with novel significance. Simply put, it is an expository narrative with Nietzschean hopes. Nietzsche is arousing the poetic imagination to narrate the rise and fall of Western metaphysics and its shift from "fact" to fable. But why tell this narrative, this slant?

To be clear, Nietzsche's death of God is interwoven with the death of metaphysics. "For Nietzsche, the *requiem aeternam deo* is likewise the *requiem aeternam mataphysicae*."[8] To compose an elegy for God meant Nietzsche needed to devote a stanza to Western metaphysics because Christian theology was a major character in the European drama. Yet, for our German philosopher, he did not *want* to "kill God," thereby throwing European society into existential crisis and social chaos. Rather, the death of God was the death of a metaphysical system that was entangled with and interwoven into Western society.

Nietzsche fully recognized that both God and metaphysics had to be transgressed so that an already-but-not-yet Nietzschean epoch could signal the pinnacle of human history.[9] Going back to his Enlightenment hopes, Nietzsche was ultimately convinced that the Christian God and the theistic metaphysic were impeding society from becoming something better,[10] and his

---

[8] A modern translation of the Latin here is "the death of God is also the death of metaphysics." See Bruce Ellis Benson, *Graven Ideologies: Nietzsche, Derrida, and Marion on Modern Idolatry* (IVP Academic, 2002), 88.

[9] A sneaky double entendre here: Nietzsche's reading of history was a *transgression* because it was rather offensive to Christian readers in his day. At the same time, his historical slant was a *transgression* because it intentionally trespassed or went beyond the historical orthodoxies of his day.

[10] In 1886, Nietzsche published *Beyond Good and Evil*, a culminating work on his revaluation of values. The subtitle of that work both

philosophical predecessors in the Enlightenment had "failed to draw the necessary, broader metaphysical and moral conclusions" to render God as "implausible and unnecessary."[11] Thus, Nietzsche's death of God is an intentional irruption of the social norms that Europe could not relinquish. According to Nietzsche, Europeans had been deluded by democratic ideologies, by a powerful majority who had spun enticing and enslaving transcendent narratives, and society cried for rescue from slavery. These transcendent narratives of Greco-Christian origins, according to Nietzsche, are not real; they are culturally manufactured idols. For Nietzsche, this domineering of metaphysics by ancient Greek and Christian figures needs to be undone because these theological and metaphysical ideologies are, at best, idols that need to be toppled.

Nietzsche was ultimately convinced that the Christian God and the theistic metaphysic were impeding society from becoming something better.

As noted in the introductory chapter, Nietzsche uses his weapon of choice, a philosophical hammer, to sound out all

captures and reveals his philosophical hope: *Prelude to a Philosophy of the Future.* As Julian Young shows in a letter between Nietzsche and his sister, Elizabeth, after *Beyond Good and Evil* he was planning on producing a four-volume masterpiece "with the fearsome title of *The Will to Power. Attempt at a Revaluation of All Values.*" See Julian Young, *Friedrich Nietzsche: A Philosophical Biography* (Cambridge University Press, 2010), 407.

[11] Carl Trueman, *The Rise and Triumph of the Modern Self: Cultural Amnesia, Expressive Individualism, and the Road to Sexual Revolution* (Crossway, 2020), 168.

cultural idols in *Twilight of the Idols.* Nietzsche believed that European society during his day clung to eternalized ideologies and idols, viewing them as absolute truths. These ideologies, often rooted in a Christian worldview, presented a skewed perspective of reality. The issue for Nietzsche was that this false perspective prevented people from truly engaging with the world and generating meaningful lives. Theology, in his view, served a sociological function and did not reveal any ultimate truths. So, when Nietzsche taps his philosophical hammer on these theological and metaphysical cultural ideologies, the seemingly eternal concepts are challenged and their emptiness is exposed, revealing their "real" worth and origins.

In summary, Nietzsche hopes to demythologize, sociologize, and psychologize God, metaphysics, and their accompanying moralities. For Nietzsche, God is a sociological projection and a deification of ideas. When we are confronted with any traditionally held narrative or moral norm, we must, says Nietzsche, see them as sociological symptoms, not as *truth*. If there is room for God, according to Nietzsche, then he must be viewed "as a maximal state, as an epoch—a point in the evolution of the will to power."[12]

Nietzsche's God in the Modern Cultural Imagination

Canadian philosopher Charles Taylor refers to how Westerners now perceive their world as a "modern social imaginary," which he defines as "the way we collectively imagine, even

[12] Nietzsche, *Will to Power*, 639.

pretheoretically, our social life in the contemporary Western world."[13] So, when I refer to a modern cultural imagination in this section and future chapters, I am intentionally and heavily borrowing from Taylor's concept.

This collective imagination has been inherited, instilled, and imbibed into a social psyche predominate among Westerners—Americans and Europeans, generally speaking. Additionally, Taylor emphasizes that these modern imaginaries are more pretheoretical rather than theoretical. Metaphorically speaking, our thoughts are driven by **epistemic** undercurrents rather than waves. To put it differently, our thoughts, ideas, and beliefs are, according to Taylor, subtly influenced by our pretheoretical desires rather than by our rational theories,[14] and these undercurrent thoughts are influenced by and carried through cultural stories and symbols.[15]

Why mention this brief digression on a modern culture imagination? As noted in the introduction, I will explain how Nietzsche has influenced our collective ways of perceiving the world in each chapter framed around the chapter's topic—whether it be God, identity, morality, truth, and so forth. It is obvious that not every Westerner has read Nietzsche or even knows who he is. Yet, his philosophy has been inherited, instilled, and imbibed within our psychological and social worlds. My aim

---

[13] See Charles Taylor, *Modern Social Imaginaries* (Duke University Press, 2004), 1.

[14] Two infamous names within this epistemological camp are Esther Meek and James K. A. Smith. See Meek's *Loving to Know: Covenant Epistemology* (Cascade, 2011) and Smith's *Desiring the Kingdom: Worship, Worldview, and Cultural Formation* (Baker Academic, 2009).

[15] Taylor, *Modern Social Imaginaries*, 1.

is to elucidate some of the ways Nietzsche is alive and well in this modern cultural imagination.

According to Nietzsche, Christianity had cast a long shadow over Europe, and it needed to be defeated so that European society could thrive. Nietzsche's concerns were primarily pragmatic.[16] He strived to elicit a new world order by purging Europe of superstitions and liberating it from religious tyrannies. Focusing so much time on theological dialogues hinders a society's progress, Nietzsche concluded. Thus, European culture had to "defeat God's shadows," if it truly desired to inaugurate a better world. However, it is important to note that Nietzsche does not have an objective or neutral vantage point here. He, too, sees perspectivally and even proposes his own *mythos*, a competing ontology and epistemology of seeing and sensing reality.[17]

Illustrating these "shadows" of God in the late eighteenth-century France—yet equally true of nineteenth-century Germany—historian Tom Holland narrates the background of Enlightenment Europe:

---

[16] Remember that Nietzsche was a trained philologist, which means he interpreted history and reality via language and the evolution of language. For instance, in *Genealogy of Morals* Nietzsche's opening essay is driven by this philological hermeneutic where concepts like "good" and "evil" are a society's subjective expressions of power. Julian Young writes, "It was [the Jews] who . . . first conquered the nobles by bringing about the replacement of noble morality's equation: 'good = noble = powerful = beautiful = happy = blessed', with slave morality's 'good = suffering = poor = powerless = lowly" (*Friedrich Nietzsche*, 461).

[17] One of Nietzsche's most well-known contributions to recent Western philosophy was his "perspectivalism." See the Glossary for a fuller definition of this term.

> The roots of Christianity stretched too deep, too thick, coiled too implacably around the foundations of everything that constituted the fabric of France, gripped too rightly its venerable and massive stonework, to be pulled up with any ease. In a realm long hailed as the eldest daughter of the Church, the ambition of setting the world on a new order, of purging it of superstition, of redeeming it from tyranny, could hardly help but be shot through with Christian assumptions.[18]

In much the same way, Nietzsche wanted to overcome God and metaphysics by dismissing or transgressing them, but as Martin Heidegger and Bruce Benson both point out: "One cannot escape philosophy—and thereby metaphysics—by making a philosophical argument against it."[19]

To reiterate, Nietzsche labors to create a new *mythos*, a new world order without the taints of Christianity (and Platonism). However, as I have been teasing thus far, when Nietzsche heralds this twilight, he cannot describe it without borrowing from the Christian narrative. Commenting on this paradox, Charles Taylor writes:

> The profoundly Christian resonance which remains paradoxically in Nietzsche in spite of his virulent opposition to Christianity lies in his aspiration to affirm the

---

[18] Tom Holland, *Dominion: How the Christian Revolution Remade the World* (Basic Books, 2019), 395.

[19] Quote from Bruce Ellis Benson, *Pious Nietzsche: Decadence and Dionysian Faith* (Indiana University Press, 2008), 38; Martin Heidegger, "The Word of Nietzsche: 'God is Dead'," in *The Question Concerning Technology and Other Essays*, trans. William Lovitt (Harper & Row, 1977), 75.

> whole of reality, to see it as good, to say "yes" to it all. . . . Everything is will to power, and humans only a more intense objectification of this will. The aspiration is realized by a victory over oneself, a kind of 'self-overcoming', in which one is able to affirm the world, even though it remains the domain of blind, unspiritual, chaotic forces.[20]

Taylor adds, "Affirming the will to power carries the will to a higher potency for Nietzsche."[21] In his denial of metaphysical realities and supernatural deities, Nietzsche does not overpower or nullify them; he ends up *deifying something else*, such as the self and the will (hence, Taylor's "higher potency" language). As Holland's quote alludes, many Enlightenment figures attempted to nudge society into new horizons but inconsistently did so *with* Christian assumptions and standards.[22]

It is not uncommon to see this deifying phenomenon captured in films today. In the 2011 movie *The Grey*, a plane crash leaves six oil workers fighting for survival against a relentless pack of wolves in the harsh Alaskan wilderness. The film, shrouded in darkness and despair, explores themes of survival, death, and the search for meaning in a seemingly indifferent universe. Liam Neeson's character, Ottway, emerges as the group's leader, his skills tested against the unforgiving elements and the constant threat of the wolves. As the men dwindle in number, Ottway finds himself alone, grappling with the weight of loss and the

---

[20] Charles Taylor, *Sources of the Self: The Making of the Modernity Identity* (Harvard University Press, 1989), 453.

[21] Taylor, *Sources of Self*, 454.

[22] Holland notes how even Voltaire, France's great (agnostic) philosopher, articulated the issues and solutions of France by the assumptions and standards of Christian Scripture. See Holland, *Dominion*, 394.

apparent absence of divine intervention. In a final act of defiance, he confronts the wolves, symbolizing humanity's struggle against the indifferent forces of a seemingly meaningless nature. This movie ultimately suggests that human existence is governed by chance and the primal laws of survival. In a world devoid of easy answers, individuals must find their own strength and purpose, even in the face of overwhelming adversity.

The Grey is more than Hollywood entertainment. It is a visual yet symbolic topography of a Nietzschean-inspired metaphysic: a world without God and even potentially one without God's shadow. In his 1882 book *The Gay Science*, Nietzsche writes, "God is dead; but given the way people are, there may still for millennia be caves in which they show his shadow. And we—we must defeat his shadow as well."[23] As illustrated previously in this chapter, Nietzsche was not merely promoting atheism as much as extending some of the Enlightenment's utilitarian goals: to master creation, to deify the individual, to generate "scientific" results, and to erect a thriving society in an age where God was becoming unbelievable.

In demoting God, says Nietzsche, man exalts himself through his own will. Offering commentary to this point, Bruce Benson states, "It would seem that the will to power is *not* a metaphysical but what we might call a *physical* principle. To shift the center of gravity back to this world and to make life central is to leave metaphysics [i.e., God] behind, which means we are left with only the physical world."[24] For instance, the premise of *Ecce Homo*

---

[23] Nietzsche, *The Gay Science: With a Prelude in Rhymes and an Appendix of Songs* (Vintage, 1984), 180.

[24] Bruce Benson, *Pious Nietzsche: Decadence and Dionysian Faith* (Indiana University Press, 2008), 37.

illustrates how themes like religion, art, and morality are not metaphysical topics but rather human phenomena. This stands in contrast with earlier German thinkers like Arthur Schopenhauer, whose "version of Kant's metaphysical idealism entails the existence of a *meta*-physical, *supra*-natural world 'beyond' or 'behind' the 'dream'-world of nature." However, for Nietzsche, "Nothing is 'behind' nature, nothing exists but nature."[25]

If, as Nietzsche proposes, there is no deeper meaning, no purpose beyond the natural world, and nothing metaphysical behind nature, then humanity is faced with a bleak and indifferent reality, where it must confront loss and the seeming lack of any higher power to guide or protect. The death of God initiates a new social order, one no longer circumnavigating God and the old moral order. Also, the death of God initiates a new moral order relocated around a competition of wills to power. This Nietzschean new world, therefore, mirrors Ottway's bleak and desolate reality, where existence is reduced to a struggle of wills, instincts, and the primal drive for survival. As much as Nietzsche remains positive and hopeful for this future, it seems to be both untenable and unlivable. Can a better and alternative narrative be told?

Creatio ex amore: Learning How to Become *Like* God

In the introductory chapter, I promised to explore some central inconsistencies and tensions within Nietzsche's writings, and in

---

[25] Young, *Friedrich Nietzsche*, 242. See also Sue Prideaux's connections between Nietzsche's philosophy and that of his friend Jacob Burckhardt in *I Am Dynamite!: A Life of Nietzsche* (Duggan, 2018), 66–71.

this section I shall attempt to elucidate a few of these. To be clear, a fundamental inconsistency within Nietzsche's theology is that he wants to overcome God-talk but still parodies the language, metaphors, themes, and narrative of Scripture to develop his own cultural narrative. As a reminder, Nietzsche desires for us to suspect that theology is ultimately sociological. In other words, he turns all God-talk into social-talk. For some Enlightenment figures—David Hume and Voltaire—it was common to presume that the sciences delivered answers and obtained true progress, whereas theology was seen as a superfluous discipline without pragmatic implications. Although Michael Gillespie comments on the rise of nihilism within the Enlightenment, we can make the same conclusion about theology: "Nihilism, as it was originally understood . . . was rather the consequence of the assertation of an absolute human will that renders God superfluous and thus for all intents and purposes dead."[26]

A fundamental inconsistency within Nietzsche's theology is that he wants to overcome God-talk but still parodies the language, metaphors, themes, and narrative of Scripture to develop his own cultural narrative.

Now, it is worth quickly noting that Nietzsche produces a positive and humbling critique for contemporary discussions pertaining to theology. The Christian can be easily tempted to idolize God-talk when he or she trusts more in a theological system than in the divine person theology points to. It is a fair critique of any theological camp

[26] Michael Allen Gillespie, *Nihilism Before Nietzsche* (University of Chicago Press, 1995), 256.

within Christianity, but it is unfair to state that *all* God-talk is essentially a sociological power play. As the introductory chapter noted, Nietzsche borrows from Ludwig Feuerbach to contend that God is a psychic projection of oneself, a deifying of the self into and onto the world. And if "God" is nothing more than an ongoing psychic event, then Nietzsche can easily locate and exalt the individual self as the site of true power and transformation. As Martin Heidegger writes regarding Nietzsche's thought, "The pronouncement 'God is dead' can be thought adequately only from out of the essence of the will to power."[27]

However, what if Nietzsche is partly right? What if sometimes God is "used" as a ploy for power? History has narrated for us dozens of examples of this.[28] Yet, in its healthiest and humblest forms, Christian theology truly desires to meet with a God who speaks and works within the mundane and immanent.

For instance, the opening scenes of Genesis reveal the themes of both creation and communion. "The garden of Eden is not viewed by the author of Genesis simply as a piece of Mesopotamian farmland, but as an archetypal sanctuary, that is a place where God dwells and where man should worship him."[29] Gordon Wenham demonstrates that the early Genesis

---

[27] Heidegger, "Word of Nietzsche," 75.

[28] The Middle Ages, Reformation, and Modern periods offer a plethora of examples: abuses of indulgences in Catholicism, inquisitional endeavors, John Calvin's permission of the trial and murder of Michael Servetus, and even Adolf Hitler's relationship with the German Catholic church. Intentionally and unintentionally, American evangelicals are also guilty of "using" God's name as power bids to collect more votes for a political party.

[29] Gordon J. Wenham, "Sanctuary Symbolism in the Garden of Eden Story," *Proceedings of the World Congress of Jewish Studies* (1985): 19.

story implants a symbolic epistemic framework within Israel that reflects how it understood itself in fellowship with this God, who created creation and humanity and revealed himself through creation and to humanity (Rom 1:20). Genesis 1–3 is more than a creation out of nothing—a *creatio ex nihilo*—it is better understood as a *creatio ex amore*. To live in God's created world was to abide in intimate, loving fellowship with this God. The opening chapters of Genesis herald a temple scene where God lovingly fashions holy spaces for humanity to reciprocate that love toward him and one another in perfect shalom.

This Hebrew word shalom is first and foremost an ontological reality. Rooted in the personhood of the triune God, shalom is God's *being* (hence ontological). God is fullness, completeness, and wholeness (Ps 18:3). God lacks nothing, and because he lacks nothing, he originally fashioned a cosmos without disorder, chaos, lack, and death: "God saw all that he had made, and it was *very* good indeed" (Gen 1:31). His original creation was ontologically "very good." It teemed with shalom. Within this creational wholeness, God creates humanity to embody his shalomic character. The fullness and completeness of God are carried in spiritual acts of devotion that have ethical, social, and political implications: "The Lord God took the man and placed him in the garden of Eden to work it and watch over it" (Gen 2:15).[30] The subtle verbs here ("work" and "watch") are for humanity to cultivate God's shalom *beyond* the boundaries of Eden, thereby

[30] The last adjective, "political," may scare some. Read properly, Gen 1–3 has political undertones, meaning this: to *live under* the rule and reign of King Yahweh-Elohim is to *live out* the rule and reign of King Yahweh-Elohim. Humans as coregents of God is an undeniable characteristic of these opening chapters.

extending Eden into all the earth, "so that God may be all in all" (1 Cor 15:28). Since the beginning, the commission for humanity has been to imitate God's shalom, which would then permeate all of creation, making the entire world an exuding presence of God, a worldwide temple.

These opening chapters of Genesis are a protological way God desires for his people to relate to his creation and their neighbors in the future, as the narrative progresses.[31] In other words, Eden is more than a place of shalomic fellowship. It functions as an epistemic, orientational way of exemplifying the transcendent within the immanent.[32] Eden gives God's people a way of seeing and being in his world. Throughout the entire scriptural storyline, Eden is always longed for. Case in point, the construction of the tabernacle (Exod 36–40) and temple (1 Kgs 6) both resonate with Edenic language. To enter both the tabernacle and the temple was to reenter Eden, a place of intimate fellowship with God. Even the prophets yearn for a restoration

---

[31] I steal the term "protological" from Jon D. Levenson, "The Temple and the World," *Journal of Religion* 64.3 (1984): 283. The Edenic temple is protological in the sense that it reveals the theological origins of Israel's (and the church's) commission and calling to abide in the presence of God.

[32] As G. K. Chesterton captured: "The great sin of mankind, the sin typified by the fall of Adam, is the tendency, not towards pride, but towards this weird and horrible humility. This is the great fall, the fall by which the fish forgets the sea, the ox forgets the meadow, the clerk forgets the city, every man forgets his environment and, in the fullest and most literal sense, forgets himself. This is the real fall of Adam, and it is a spiritual fall. It is a strange thing that many truly spiritual men, such as General Gordon, have actually spent some hours in speculating upon the precise location of the Garden of Eden. Most probably we are in Eden still. It is only our eyes that have changed." See Chesterton, *The Defendant: Original Classics and Annotated* (Pranava, 2022), 11.

of Eden (Ezek 40–43). In fact, Eden bookends the entire story of Scripture. As Scripture begins, it tells the tale of intimate presence, fellowship, and communion, and when the story closes in Rev 21–22, Eden is remembered, reinstituted, and resurrected where "God's dwelling is [*again*] with humanity" (Rev 21:3).[33]

Returning to Nietzsche, he invites European (and Western) culture to attune its life to his tuning fork that has two prongs: the first prong of sheer will to power and the second prong of a heroic individualism. For Nietzsche, God-talk and metaphysical-talk are distracting and superfluous to the real and obligatory concerns of European society, and thus the self becomes central for Nietzsche, because it is in and through the self that physical society can be changed.[34] As outlined in this chapter, to generate a future world without God requires both tuning prongs. For Nietzsche, human volition and individualism can arrest a new world order. We must move beyond the transcendent, the metaphysical, and the divine to embrace the immanent, the physical, and the mundane. The myth of Genesis, says Nietzsche, must be subverted to inaugurate a life-affirming philosophy (and science!) that affirms the here and now and not an unseen afterworld. In order to attain his hopeful future, Nietzsche says we must detach our lives from such theological myths. However, Gen 1–3 attests to an inherent "doxological self" we cannot escape or thwart: A self that is undeniably and intrinsically worshipful, which has been created by a communal three-in-one

---

[33] The echoes of Gen 1–3 in Rev 21–22 are too abundant to footnote here. I prod you to read the narratives for themselves. For further study, see G. K. Beale, *The Temple and the Church's Mission: A Biblical Theology of the Dwelling Place of God* (IVP Academic, 2004).

[34] Nietzsche, *Ecce Homo*, 95.

God for the purpose of communal doxology. Commenting on these opening scenes in Gen 1–3, Chris Watkin writes, "It is no exaggeration to say that in the Trinity the Bible gives us an ontology of love, that for a Christian Trinitarian view, love is 'the original law of human social being,' and that violence is its negation."[35] The concept of love implies the existence of both a lover and something/someone loved. As Michael Hanby captures, "The doxological self is thus able to participate in the life of the Trinity by virtue of a doxological character which it cannot escape, but can only pervert."[36]

The myth that Nietzsche wants to sabotage is twofold: first the doxological nature of humanity, and second the triune God. In Augustinian tradition, God is "the loving one and what is loved and love."[37] But contrary to Nietzsche's views, God is not a projection and deification of ideas; this means that Nietzsche's democratic, demagogical, and deification theses are not "objective," scientific truths. Again, his philosophical theses are a *mythos*—his own metanarrative of history that we are justified in discounting. In other words, Nietzsche parodies the creation story of Genesis by instituting a new creation story where God is not denied but metamorphized. Supreme power, once located

---

[35] Watkin, *Biblical Critical Theory*, 50.

[36] Michael Hanby, "Desire: Augustine Beyond Western Subjectivity" in *Radical Orthodoxy: A New Theology*, ed. John Milbank, Catherine Pickstock, and Graham Ward (Routledge, 1999), 115.

[37] Augustine, *Confessions*, trans. Henry Chadwick (Oxford University Press, 1991), 311. In its fuller context, Augustine articulates a triune theology of love: "Behold, I who seek this, when I love something, there are three, I and what I love and the love itself. Indeed, I don't love love unless I love loving, for there is no love where nothing is loved. Therefore there are three, the loving one and what is loved and love" (9).

in a transcendent deity, can now be found in humanity through its will and heroism. Additionally, through this spiritual pathway of God-like will and heroics, eternal life is actualized for the self, and as a result the self becomes exalted, praised, and worshipped. For Nietzsche, *human beings have become gods*, and thus even he cannot narrate a genesis for European society without deities and doxologies.

In conclusion, Genesis commissions humanity to become like God, which is categorically different than becoming God-like, as Nietzsche wants to entertain.[38] According to Genesis, the former is the invitation of a providential God, whereas the latter is the invitation of a prudent serpent.

---

[38] In *Rise and Triumph of the Modern Self*, Carl Trueman states, "In killing God, you take on the responsibility—the terrifying responsibility—of being god yourself, of becoming the author of your own knowledge and your own ethics" (170).

Chapter 3

The *Imago Dei*: Humanity and the Will to Power (On Identity)

More than two millennia before Nietzsche, Western culture drew certain indistinguishable connections between God and human beings. Both Roman Catholic and Protestant theologians read scriptural texts like Genesis 1–3 and developed theological concepts like the *imago Dei*, "the image of God," to signify the relational, ontological, and functional connections between God and human beings. As Marc Cortez writes regarding the biblical notion of the image of God, "The key terms—*selem* and *demut* in the Old Testament, and *eikon* in the New Testament—all refer to the idea that some object reflects and resembles another in some way."[1] With his father being a pastor and having a rich theological education in the Lutheran tradition, Nietzsche was acutely aware of these biblical connections. He also clearly understood the philosophical, social, and existential implications

[1] Marc Cortez, *Theological Anthropology: A Guide for the Perplexed* (T&T Clark, 2010), 16.

of the death of God and for what it meant to be human. Even though he had hesitations about the implications, he welcomed them. He found something mysteriously exhilarating about moving beyond the Greco-Christian philosophical and historical foundations that structured and organized Western society.

In chapter 1, I outlined a Nietzschean theology to put him in conversation with the compelling theological vision of Genesis 1–3. As we saw, Nietzsche was a philosophical impetus for how the West has come to imagine (or not imagine) God in our cultural moment. In this chapter, I will illustrate how Nietzsche's dismantling of God disassembled what it means to be human. Nietzsche believed that to be human was to be self-empowering and beyond traditional kinds of being. But if God is dead, then what are the ramifications of the *imago Dei*? If the *imago Dei* is a religious farce (per Nietzsche), what does it mean to be human *now*? In short, what is a Nietzschean human? Beginning with the latter, we will explore these questions to see how Nietzsche understood the human being in the shadow of God's death. Toward this chapter's conclusion, we will explore some implications of his writings with particular attention to what it means to be human after Nietzsche.

A Short History of Essentialism: Souls, Spirits, and What It Means to Be Human

For Greek-minded philosophers like Aristotle, Socrates, or Plato, to be human meant to have an undeniable essence.[2] Both

[2] On Aristotle's stance, see Marguerite Deslauriers and Zoli Filotas, "Aristotle's Human Beings," in *Human: A History*, Karolina Hubner (Oxford University Press, 2022).

the ancient Greek and Christian positions promote a type of **essentialism** where humans have intrinsic attributes characterizing their identity, such as a soul or rationality. To deny these essential characteristics is to deny what it means to be human according to commonly held Western categories. Christian theology through the centuries suggested that to be human was to be an image bearer of God, which signified some type of relational, ontological, or functional connection between God and his image-bearing agents.

If there's one work that develops Nietzsche's notion of the human, it is *Ecce Homo*. This Latin phrase is taken from Pilate's exclamation of Jesus in John 19:5, "Here is the man!" Rather than affirming any Chalcedonian view of Jesus,[3] Nietzsche subverts this theologically orthodox stance to de-deify Jesus making him a mere human unworthy of devotion and worship, making him more of a paradigm to follow. In doing so, Nietzsche immanentizes the transcendent; he's purposefully profaning the holy.

As noted throughout this work, Greco-Roman and Christian narratives predominated the cultural, social, and philosophical cultures of the West in the eighteenth and nineteenth centuries, especially Germany. For Nietzsche, Europeans must leave

---

[3] The Chalcedonian Creed affirms the following about Jesus's fully divine yet fully human nature "begotten before all ages of the Father according to the Godhead, and in these latter days, for us and for our salvation, born of the Virgin Mary, the mother of God, according to the manhood; one and the same Christ, Son, Lord, Only-begotten, to be acknowledged in two natures, without confusion, without change, without division, without separation; the distinction of natures being by no means taken away by the union, but rather the property of each nature being preserved, and concurring in one person and one subsistence, not parted or divided into two persons, but one and the same Son, and only begotten, God the Word, the Lord Jesus Christ."

behind these antiquated ideologies that have made us sick for "*healthier* concepts and values" and, in so doing, become "masters" of ourselves.[4] Nietzsche wants to upend these cultural forces to introduce an alternative way, and *Ecce Homo* is Nietzsche's alternative manifesto.

As Nicholas D. More has rightly concluded, *Ecce Homo* is a satirical work meant to offer a different perspective for the European worldview.[5] He writes, "Aggressive denunciation is one of satire's dominant and oldest forms, and the book's title invokes the Christian model of humanity in order to present Nietzsche's philosophy against it."[6] Greco-Roman and Christian perspectives exalted logic and rhetoric as some means of demonstrating what was true, good, and beautiful. Intentionally not utilizing these approaches, Nietzsche crafts *Ecce Homo* as a work of satire to denounce aggressively the comedic absurdity of the Christian model of humanity. In doing so, Nietzsche announces that European culture has now reached the limits of its former humanity. A new human must be born without any Greco-Roman or Christian imaginings or influences. These former narratives are to be challenged by showing what they truly are: distortions and deformations of our true humanity. Since God is dead, the self is all that remains.

---

[4] Nietzsche, *Ecce Homo: How to Become What You Are*, trans. Duncan Large (Oxford University Press, 2009), 8.

[5] More notes that satire "employs a preponderance of wit and exaggeration over logic and argumentation; it strives to make its object stupid or laughable, not prove it untrue, and uses art to entertain its readers, not bore them into rational submission." See Nicholas D. More, *Nietzsche's Last Laugh: Ecce Homo as Satire* (University of Cambridge Press, 2014), 27.

[6] More, *Nietzsche's Last Laugh*, 42.

Despite being autobiographical in its orientation, *Ecce Homo* features Nietzsche extrapolating his life as indicative of the entire human experience.[7] What we will notice is that Nietzsche was advocating for the kind of human that much of European society was beginning to entertain: a Darwinian "spin" on humanity.[8] With Nietzsche's denial of God and metaphysics, his closed immanent frame requires a particular spin on what it means to be human. In the upcoming sections, I will attempt to uncover Nietzsche's human, especially in conversation with the transcendent, open framework inherent within Christian Scripture and theology. But this raises the question for Nietzsche: "How can we become what we are?"[9]

Nietzsche's *Non imago Dei*

"Out of this work [*Ecce Homo*] speaks an immense hope," writes Nietzsche.[10] In order to birth hope for (a new) humanity, Nietzsche believed a radical shift must happen—new life must come through death. For Nietzsche, this death is the death of

---

[7] Nietzsche recognizes the significance of *Ecce Homo* as a "bookend" to his other works in the 1880s. Even though he was devising other projects before his mental decline in the 1890s, *Ecce Homo* is the last in his canon (1888), yet it logically and philosophically follows *Twilight of Idols* and *Genealogy of Morals*. He makes this point evident in the last paragraph of the foreword of *Ecce Homo*.

[8] See James K. A. Smith, *How (Not) to Be Secular: Reading Charles Taylor* (Eerdmans, 2014), 143. Smith describes a "spin" as "a construal of life within the *immanent frame* that does not recognize itself as a construal and thus has no room to grant plausibility to the alternative. [It] can be either 'closed' (immanentist) or 'open' (to transcendence)."

[9] This question echoes the subtitle of *Ecce Homo*.

[10] Nietzsche, *Ecce Homo*, 48.

being. As noted in the last chapter, Nietzsche fully recognized the future he was willing and wanting. To kill God meant the end of Western metaphysics, which likewise entailed the death of humanity, or at least the *Western idea of humanity* with all its metaphysical baggage.

To birth this hope, Nietzsche holds that we must be willing to take an epic journey, one "with a radical rejection of even the concept of 'being.'" Instead of holding on to any Greco-Roman doctrines of humanity—such as Aristotelian essentialism, Platonic notions of the soul, or Christian doctrines of the *imago Dei*—the next and necessary steps require the "doctrine of 'eternal recurrence.'"[11] But before we get into this doctrine, let us first pause to develop some preliminary ideas.

The philosophical exploration of being is known as **ontology**, a conceptual stepcousin to metaphysics. The field of ontology covers a wide range of topics, including the reality of God, existence itself, numbers, objects, universals, and even truth itself. Take, for instance, the existence of numbers. Numbers are abstract and intangible yet seem to have real existence. Numbers are transcultural realities; they are represented and communicated across all space and time regardless of culture, region, or ethnicity. In each linguistic ecosystem, we use written symbols (i.e., the numbers 1, 3, 55, or 260) that represent those abstract realities. These are semi-tangible symbols because we can actually see the number "1" on this sheet of paper, yet these written symbols somehow mysteriously point to intangible universals. As a discipline, ontology attempts to reckon with such existences. Translating ontology to questions

---

[11] Nietzsche, *Ecce Homo*, 48.

like "What does it mean to be human?" raises one of the issues Nietzsche is pursuing.

For him, God is the philosophical thread tying together all that is. If God exists, then all that exists is because of him, and everything, to some extent, participates in his being. Said differently, things *possess as well as participate in being*. But, since God does not exist for Nietzsche, thereby everything that exists is ontologically disentangled from God. As this chapter's introduction noted, if God, the Being of all beings, does not exist, then humans have no being, no essence, and no nature, thus leaving the door wide open to new possibilities of what it means to be human.[12] In particular, as Nietzsche claims, this entails that "one has to know *who* one is."[13] But to do this, according to Nietzsche, one must possess understanding of his notions of will to power and eternal recurrence. These two Nietzschean concepts are not only interconnected, but they are also extremely important throughout his oeuvre.[14] In order to be acquainted with both in connection to Nietzsche's conceptualization of the human, let us engage with each term in turn.

First, contrary to a long-held valorization of theology as the "queen of the sciences," Nietzsche firmly believed that psychology

---

[12] "Being" (uppercase) refers to the fundamental nature of existence itself, the ultimate reality, or the ground of all being. In contrast, "being" (lowercase) refers to a specific entity or thing that exists, like a tree or a person. Essentially, "Being" is the metaphysical condition for anything to exist, while "being" describes individual existents.

[13] Nietzsche, *Twilight of the Idols and the Anti-Christ*, trans. R. J. Hollingdale, ed. Michael Tanner (Penguin, 1990), 82.

[14] Nietzsche even boasted in *Thus Spoke Zarathustra* that these topics were the most important thoughts that ever came to him. For a biographical angle on these themes in his mature philosophy, see Young, *Friedrich Nietzsche*, 318–20.

was *now* the queen of the sciences,[15] and this physiological-psychology could better "plumb [the] depths" of the "moral prejudices" of the Greek and Christian worldviews that permeated the European world.[16] According to Nietzsche, once these abhorrent worldviews were exposed as "harmful, inhibiting, binding, distorting," then humanity could discover a "new realm of dangerous insights" fundamental to the human condition, which is an "evolutionary theory of the will to power."[17] Nietzsche biographer Julian Young refers to the will to power as having three interwoven doctrines: a psychological doctrine, a biological doctrine, and a cosmological doctrine.[18] Let's move from the latter to the former to better understand Nietzsche's take on these doctrines.

The cosmological doctrine of the will to power portrays all existence, "in so far as an energy is active in [it]," as mechanical, materialized energy.[19] Thus, if this is true of all organic cosmic life, then we could "designate *all* effective energy unequivocally as: the *will to power*. The world as it is seen from the inside, the world defined and described by its 'intelligible character'—would be simply 'will to power' and that alone."[20] At its very "essence," cosmic life heralds a generating force that not only underlies all

---

[15] Nietzsche, *Beyond Good and Evil: Prelude to a Philosophy of the Future*, trans. Marion Faber (Oxford University Press, 1998), 24.

[16] Nietzsche, *Beyond Good and Evil*, 23.

[17] Nietzsche, *Beyond Good and Evil*, 23. As an interpretive side-note, many Americans see "evolution" through Darwinian lenses, yet Nietzsche probably meant something closer to a *developmental* theory of the will to power. Remember that Nietzsche sees time as moving through epochal ages, hence a developing humanity who understands what it really is.

[18] Young, *Friedrich Nietzsche*, 542–49.

[19] Nietzsche, *Beyond Good and Evil*, 36.

[20] Nietzsche, *Beyond Good and Evil*, 36.

existence but also beckons for all inorganic, organic, and psychological existence to conform themselves to this exerting will to power over the Other.

Second, the biological doctrine of the will to power develops the notion that even organic and inorganic life is essentially will to power. In *Beyond Good and Evil*, Nietzsche writes, "Life itself in its essence means appropriating, injuring, overpowering those who are foreign and weaker; oppression, harshness, forcing one's own forms on others, incorporation, and at the very least, at the very mildest, exploitation."[21] Even within the biological world, Nietzsche says we see organisms exerting oppressive, exploitive forces over other weaker organisms. Such an organic force will "gain the upper hand—not out of some morality or immorality, but because it is *alive*, and because life simply *is* the will to power."[22] Here Nietzsche palpably insists that to be fully alive is to exert a will to power over the Other.

Finally, the psychological doctrine of the will to power is an extension of one's psyche; it is an internal power struggle to liberate oneself from Greco-Christian narratives, morals, and metaphysics. The human, then, is meant to live an ascending, flourishing life aimed for "growth, for the accumulation of force, of *power*."[23] Participation in this aliveness is to become who one truly is: a psychological will properly aligned to both the biological and cosmological wills to power.

According to Nietzsche, the world as we know it is not filled with an Aristotelian *eudaemonia* (happiness) where

---

[21] Nietzsche, *Beyond Good and Evil*, 153.

[22] Nietzsche, *Beyond Good and Evil*, 153.

[23] Quote from the Hollingdale translation of Nietzsche, *Anti-Christ*, 129.

human beings discover their true causes,[24] and it is certainly not defined by any God-ordained purpose to glorify and enjoy him forever.[25] Those are the ancient, cruder categories of Western philosophy and theology. A new age of the human being has dawned. The world as we know it is "described by . . . the 'will to power' and that alone."[26] From its cosmological largeness to the inner psyche, the will to power rules and defines the human being.

With a better understanding of the will to power before us, let us turn to eternal recurrence. Nietzsche develops the notion of eternal recurrence in order to define a new notion of being. As Gillespie puts it, "The purpose of this idea . . . is to provide a new notion of eternity in a nihilistic world in which the old god has died and consequently in which the old eternity has also become unbelievable."[27] Adding historical texture to this statement, Gillespie rightly notes:

---

[24] On Aristotle's four causes, see Andrea Falcon, "Aristotle on Causality," *Stanford Encyclopedia of Philosophy*, last updated March 7, 2023, https://plato.stanford.edu/entries/aristotle-causality/.

[25] An explicit nod to the Westminster Shorter Catechism Question 1: "What is the chief end of man? Answer: Man's chief end is to glorify God and enjoy him forever."

[26] Nietzsche, *Beyond Good and Evil*, 36.

[27] Michael Allen Gillespie, *Nietzsche's Final Teaching* (University of Chicago Press, 2017), 15. Following Gillespie's argument, I understand Nietzsche's eternal recurrence as focusing primarily on fashioning new ontological categories. Nietzsche sees clear connections between theism, metaphysics, and ontology, and when the first is discredited, a new anti-metaphysics, ontology, and even morality is necessary. Undoubtedly, theology, metaphysics, ontology, and morality are the resonating themes in Nietzsche's mature philosophy from 1881–1888. See Gillespie, *Nietzsche's Final Teaching*, 13–23.

> From Nietzsche's point of view, European metaphysics had become unbelievable for a variety of reasons. Traditional ontological notions had melted away in the face of early modernity skepticism that overturned belief in the existence of substantial forms. While this skepticism was itself overcome by the new science developed by Copernicus, Kepler, Galileo, Descartes, and Newton that demonstrated that change itself followed lawful and mathematically demonstrable patterns, the certitude on which it rested was called into question in the late eighteenth and early nineteenth century by historicism. In this way, by the middle of the nineteenth century, many thinkers had become convinced that the ontology and logic that had sustained the European tradition since Plato was built on sand.[28]

In many ways, Nietzsche's idea of eternal recurrence represents the next logical step in his thought process. If God is dead, then Being is dead, and if Being is dead, then being is dead. This entails that "human being," which is rooted in these metaphysical and theological concepts, is also a dead concept. For Nietzsche, this means that we are not human *beings* but rather human *becomings*, and hence the notion of **eternal recurrence** (also referred to as **eternal return**). This idea of eternal recurrence reflects Nietzsche's idea that all cosmological events repeat themselves in the exact same sequence through an eternal series of cycles. In short, one's past will reoccur into one's eternal future, again and again and again.

In many ways, the idea of eternal recurrence finds a helpful analogy in the 1993 film *Groundhog Day*. In this movie, the main

---

[28] Gillespie, *Nietzsche's Final Teaching*, 17.

character, sneering weatherman Phil Connors (Bill Murray), mysteriously finds himself reliving Groundhog Day over and over again. After accepting this daily loop, he begins to use this day for personal gain and selfish pursuits. Eventually, he seems to give up, slowly moving into despair and even attempts suicide—only to wake up and start over on February 2 again. Eventually, Phil realizes he must find meaning in this seemingly meaningless existence. As Phil asks in the film, "What would you do if you were stuck in one place and every day was exactly the same, and nothing that you did mattered?" So, he learns new abilities, begins to selflessly help others and connect with fellow human beings, like his coworker Rita. Once Phil accepts and embraces this meaningful living in the midst of meaningless time loops, the loop stops, and Phil wakes up finally on February 3. Along these lines, *Groundhog Day* can be considered a Hollywood parable of Nietzsche's eternal recurrence.

As Gillespie concisely summarizes Nietzsche on the matter, "There is no being for [Nietzsche], there is only becoming, but it is an eternal becoming of a finite set of possibilities and thus a becoming that Nietzsche believed inevitably had and has to repeat itself."[29] Even though Nietzsche denies God, he is cognizant that he must hang on to some grade of eternality, because eternalness (whether pagan or theistic) generates meaning and purpose—two categories Nietzsche will not completely let go of—as we will explore in the next chapter.

In sum, for Nietzsche, the human must be reminded where he is in history: It is nearing the Great Noon, a time where humans can meaningfully start to become. Unlike past historical

---

[29] Gillespie, *Nietzsche's Final Teaching*, 18–19.

epochs rooted in Greco-Christian ontologies, this approaching Great Noon will liberate ontology from its former metaphysical constraints, so the human can discover true liberation via the will to power.[30]

Nietzsche's Human in the Modern Cultural Imagination

Commenting on the reception of Nietzsche in America, Jennifer Ratner-Rosenhagen notes how philosophers Harold Bloom, Richard Rorty, and Stanley Cavell have employed particular Nietzschean ideas for specific philosophical purposes. Ratner-Rosenhagen writes, "Their Nietzsche harkened back to earlier philosophical interpretations which understood that in a world without foundations, our views of truth, language, and the self are not mirrors of reality but useful fictions to explore new avenues of discovery, new sources of wonder."[31] Utilizing a metallurgic metaphor, we might say that the human has become completely malleable—a perpetually self-creating and self-discovering entity. In Nietzschean language, one is no longer a human being but a human *becoming.* If we retain the old sheaths of Greco-Christian metaphysics,[32] we move backward toward essences and natures,

---

[30] Speaking of traditional ontologies (e.g., any body-soul dualism found in Platonic and Christian doctrines), Nietzsche vehemently denied these prior doctrines. He writes, "We philosophers are not free to divide body from soul as the people do." See Nietzsche, *The Gay Science*, trans. Walter Kaufmann (Vintage, 1974), 3.

[31] Jennifer Ratner-Rosenhagen, *American Nietzsche: A History of an Icon and His Ideas* (University of Chicago Press, 2012), 304.

[32] Tom Holland has historically and thematically demonstrated how Christian theology remade the Western world as we know it.

which are stagnant, unattainable, and honestly, mere fables. To move forward is to progress, thereby closing the philosophical doors on metaphysical essences, which then opens the existential doors to discovering our *becoming* selves. To live, for Nietzsche, is both an art and an act of self-discovery.

But does Nietzsche really make as clean and crisp a break from the Christian narrative as he'd like us to presume? It is important to observe here that Nietzsche's (future) human being parodies the Christian narrative in several ways, especially pertaining to its ontology and its doctrines on the *imago Dei*. First, as any introductory course on ontology would teach us, *becoming* always already presupposes some form of *being*. It is like expecting midnight's dark without the darkening shades of dusk. Likewise, becoming presumes certain concepts of being. As outlined in the previous section, Nietzsche deeply desired a future without being while assuming certain concepts about being, such as ancient Greek and Christian theories of being. Martin Heidegger, for instance, critiqued Nietzsche here by claiming that the radical German anti-theist and anti-metaphysician could not completely disband himself from traditional notions of theistic metaphysics.[33] The Christian narrative develops an overarching story of humankind, the bearers of the *imago Dei*, who, despite their fallenness, undergo a spiritual journey toward becoming the bearers of the resurrected *imago Dei* (1 John 3:2).

In his preface he writes, "This book explores what it was that made Christianity so subversive and disruptive; how completely it came to saturate the mindset of Latin Christendom; and why, in a West that is often doubtful of religion's claims, so many of its instincts remain—for good and ill—thoroughly Christian." See Holland, *Dominion: How the Christian Revolution Remade the World* (Basic Books, 2019), 17.

[33] See Martin Heidegger, *Nietzsche*, 2 vols. (Neske, 1961), 1:648–58.

In short, Nietzsche plagiarized this narrative by suggesting the current human being is not who he or she truly is, and he thereby supposed that we are becoming (or should master ourselves) to become something more.

Second, Nietzsche steals from the Christian narrative where human beings are divinely commissioned to steward and have dominion over creation (Gen 1:26–28) and then substitutes this divine commission with a self-commission—a type of autonomy focused on the self.[34] Charles Taylor refers to this way of interpreting the world as "exclusive humanism," which is an attempt to see and sense the world without any divine or transcendent planes. When the gods are "displaced as the centre of social life," then meaning can only be discovered within the present, immanent, and horizontal plane. Mastery of self is a defining theme in Nietzsche's later writings, thus further solidifying his status as a poster child of modernity. Numerous figures within the Enlightenment—from Francis Bacon to René Descartes to Immanuel Kant—spilled considerable amounts of ink on the ideal of humanity's domineering control over nature. But this theme of dominion becomes largely *internalized* within Nietzsche's writings, thus generating, as developed earlier in this chapter, his doctrine of the will to power.

Commenting on the Enlightenment's fetish with the mastery of creation and the self, John Milbank writes, "One important aspect of modernity was the sense that human beings could make and remake their own cultural universe. . . . Because humans were also recognized as natural, such [fixed] laws [of nature] were seen as impinging on the human sphere also—limiting the range

---

[34] See Charles Taylor, *A Secular Age* (Harvard University Press, 2007), 18–20.

of freedom for self-making."[35] Nietzsche's philosophical mission was not novel or innovative. Rather, as we have seen, his hopeful narrative parodied a Christian ontology and its accompanying humanism: A world already filled with creaturely beings who yearn to become something more (Rom 8:18–21).

Tracing this Nietzschean-infused self-making into our modern age, Milbank adds, "No longer are there firm characteristics of childhood, middle or old age; no longer are there clearly any men and women, less and less is there much acutely bounded heterosexuality as opposed to the single, univocal . . . proliferation of multiple desires."[36] Although Milbank's quote was published in 2004, more than twenty years before the printing of this book, it still rings true today. Across Europe and North America, we could indisputably speak about the cultural explosion of this enchantment with self-discovery and self-creation. With the invitation of Nietzsche, the human is invited on an existential journey "to explore new avenues of discovery, new sources of wonder," and even new identities.[37]

Nietzsche believed he was a philosophical contributor for future Western societies to fashion new identities. Undoubtedly, the body has become a battleground in the twentieth and twenty-first centuries. Various communities have consecrated the body as something *more than* the moorings of a Christianized humanity and to welcome new horizons of what it means to be human. As Andrew Root winsomely writes, "To 'welcome' is not just to allow but to affirm the performance the self is undertaking (and

---

[35] John Milbank, *Being Reconciled: Ontology and Pardon* (Routledge, 2004), 188.

[36] Milbank, *Being Reconciled*, 188.

[37] Ratner-Rosenhagen, *American Nietzsche*, 304.

the possibilities of its magnificence). Welcoming means much more than just the absence of prohibition; it means real embrace of distinct performances of unique identities."[38] The spirit of Nietzsche is alive and well within Western culture. More importantly, the *Geist* of Nietzsche has enlivened Western culture with its efforts to liberate itself from "static" essences, natures, and laws to pursue freely the innumerable horizons of possibility—especially the boundless possibilities of human identity, sexuality, and technology.

To conclude this section, let us belabor Nietzsche's logic one more time. If God is dead, so is the *imago Dei*. If the *imago Dei* is dead, then the human is not a human being (in any Christian sense) but an endless possibility of human becomings. Like Phil Connors, life is nothing but an endless, meaningless loop, prompting us to ask, "What would you do if you were stuck in one place and every day was exactly the same, and nothing that you did mattered?" To answer this question, Nietzsche says that the human becomes a blank slate. He breaks the cultural soil for future Western societies to fashion new identities, and such a future *seems* to be filled with wonder.

Beings and Bodies: Learning How to Become Human

To tie the preceding and current chapters together, once Nietzsche kills God, the theologically designed identity associated with God (*imago Dei*) expires, which causes the will to

---

[38] Andrew Root, *The Church in an Age of Secular Mysticisms: Why Spiritualities Without God Fail to Transform Us* (Baker Academic, 2023), 30.

be relocated as the new dawn of self-expressive identity. For Scripture, being and bodies are intimately connected to identity. Nietzsche does not disagree with this, yet he wants these former theological myths to be transcended for fresh possibilities of what it means to be human. Modern cultural philosophies even envision the body as a habitation for identity formation. Our bodies are teased to find identity in consumerism, nationalism, militarism, transgenderism, Nietzscheanism, or whatever the novel -ism of the day is. If Christians affirm the human being as an *imago Dei*, then Nietzsche affirms the negative: The human is a *non imago Dei*—the not-divine image—in ontology, function, or representation.[39]

Twentieth-century American philosophers, like Richard Rorty and Harold Bloom, "believed, as so many before them had, that a world 'after Nietzsche' need not be a world without wonder. While Nietzsche provided (post-) modern Americans with neither compass nor guide for the moral life, he also demonstrated to them that a life without meaning is not a life worth living."[40] To rephrase Ratner-Rosenhagen, she suggests that Nietzsche's quest was to nurture a social order with new wonderments yet without Christian, transcendental categories. Nietzsche urged humankind to hope for a better, forthcoming humanity, and he even bid Europe to wonder with excitement over these possibilities. So, how can the church embody a rich theological anthropology in our Nietzschean age—an age that wants wonder without Greco-Christian categories?

---

[39] On the various angles of what it means to be in the *imago Dei*, such as ontological, functional, or representative image bearing, see Cortez, *Theological Anthropology*.

[40] Ratner-Rosenhagen, *American Nietzsche*, 305.

In his first epistle, John writes, "But we know that when he appears, we will be like him because we will see him as he is" (1 John 3:2). John, as a representative of the wider apostolic imagination (Paul in 1 Cor 15 and Peter in 2 Pet 3), understands Jesus's resurrected body as the fleshly blueprint of a future cosmic resurrection event. It is what Paul calls the "first fruits" (1 Cor 15:20–23) or a now-but-not-yet foretaste of a future global reality (Rom 8:20–25). Unquestionably, the entire biblical canon is concerned with the human body: from creation to fall to gardening to ritual to masonry to menstruation to resting to liberation to drinking to working to farming to sex to murder to listening to loving to incarnation to following to feeding to feasting to crucifixes and to resurrection.

> It is not an exaggeration to state that the human body is a highly valuable asset within God's created ecology and his redemptive economy.

The human being exists to imitate her creator, and she is commissioned to em*body* God's salvation. The human being is the nexus where the divine and human body meet, and thus the human being is the enfleshed locus where doxology happens.

Reflecting on a theology of the body, Graham Ward writes that if the "eucharistic and Christic body informs all other understandings of 'body' for Christian teaching: then what kind of bodies is Christianity concerned with?"[41] Those of you from baptistic or free church traditions may be concerned with Ward's emphasis upon the Eucharist, yet his point is valid: The

[41] Graham Ward, *Cities of God* (Routledge, 2000), 83.

incarnation and resurrected body of Christ not only inform all other understandings of body but also inform all other understandings of being (read: ontology). Said differently, "Christic" being and embodiment should influence how we understand the notions of being and bodies, or as Paul writes to the church at Colossae:

> [Christ] is the image of the invisible God, . . .
> For everything was created by him,
> in heaven and on earth, the visible and the invisible, . . .
> all things have been created through him and for him.
> He is before all things,
> and by him all things hold together.
> He is also the head of the body, the church (Col 1:15–18).

Here Paul weaves together Christology, ontology, and identity. The church discovers its truest identity, its nature, and its purpose through unity with Christ. As Marianne Meye Thompson observes, "The church of which Christ is the head is humanity as it was created to be. Paul thus draws a parallel between Christ's role in creation and his role as head of the church. As the head of his body, the church, Christ is its source or beginning and its life and therefore rightfully has preeminence in it."[42]

In conclusion, allow me to quote the always poetically winsome Augustine, who wrote:

> Late have I loved you, O Beauty ever ancient, ever new, late have I loved you! You were within me, but I was outside, and it was there that I searched for you. In my

---

[42] Marianne Meye Thompson, Colossians and Philemon, *The Two Horizons New Testament Commentary* (William B. Eerdmans, 2005), 33.

> unloveliness I plunged into the lovely things which you created. You were with me, but I was not with you. Created things kept me from you; yet if they had not been in you, they would not have been at all. You called, you shouted, and you broke through my deafness. You flashed, you shone, and you dispelled my blindness. You breathed your fragrance on me; I drew in breath and now I pant for you. I have tasted you, now I hunger and thirst for more. You touched me, and I burned for your peace.[43]

Augustine wrestles and weeps over coming to the knowledge of Christ late in his life, and ever so eloquently he refers to Christ as Beauty itself. For Augustine, to know Christ is to be changed into a new humanity made fully alive: "You breathed your fragrance on me; I drew in breath and now I pant for you. I have tasted you, now I hunger and thirst for more. You touched me, and I burned for your peace." Even though unbeautiful and unlovely things once "kept [him] from [Christ]," it is in the knowing of Christ that Augustine has been enabled to see what's truly beautiful: "you dispelled my blindness."

Through his quote, Augustine captures his own personal experiences, and he also illuminates a profound biblical connection between God and the *imago Dei* and thus the correlation between one's design, nature, and identity. Scripture teaches that to know the triune God is to know oneself. Or more concisely, to know God is to become fully human. Again, Nietzsche challenged this "static," traditional view of human nature, envisioning us as beings in constant flux, perpetually becoming something

---

[43] Augustine. *Confessions*, trans. Henry Chadwick (Oxford University Press, 1991), 201.

else without *imago Dei* language. His perspective rejects the supposed rigid confines of Christian metaphysics and ontology, opening the door to an existential exploration of self-creation and self-discovery. For Nietzsche, we are not defined by divinely created essences but instead by the ongoing process of becoming. Nietzsche aspires to introduce this new identity for humanity through *his* knowledge, which he saw as revelatory for Europe and the West. Ironically, Nietzsche's hope parodies an infamous biblical scene, where humans were tempted with a radically new identity, but with this new identity, humans must be willing to disconnect and disfellowship themselves from God. But this unorthodox and revelatory knowing is not delivered by a snake in a garden but by Nietzsche himself, which bridges us to the next chapter on the fall.

Chapter 4

The Fall: *Décadence*, Decay, and Death (On Morality and Meaning)

As we surveyed in the previous two chapters, Nietzsche understood that if God is considered the Value of all values, then he has fashioned and formed creation with inherent value. Our lives are to be moral, and our daily living is laced with meaning. But if God is dead, then what can be said of morality and of a meaningful life? Nietzsche vigorously worked to upend Western theism and metaphysics by revealing it to be a farce and a fable. Underneath these former systems were powers positioned to enslave society, and human "beings" were being deceived by these oppressive powers that ultimately caused ***décadence***.[1]

[1] Any way of life—philosophy, religion, art—that proclaims weakness is considered *décadent*. Oftentimes, Nietzsche prefers the French word *décadent* to describe moralities and modes of life that announce weakness as the way. Julian Young writes, "Nietzsche takes over the term—which from now on becomes his favourite summation of all that is wrong with modernity—from the French literary movement of the late nineteenth century personified by Baudelaire's *Fleur du mal*,

Nietzsche understood decadent moralities as types of psychological neuroses, because those who love such moralities slowly die by them.[2] Such individuals are neurotic because they crave what kills them. Hence, for Nietzsche, morality was at stake in the Western world,[3] and as he rightly understood, morality is not merely a system of beliefs one carries around in one's head. Better understood, morality is a way of life; *it's a valued embodiment.* Since the old Greco-Christian epoch is passing away and the Great Noon approaches, we need both a revaluation and a transvaluation of values. Alongside a new metaphysics (chapter 1) and a new anthropology (chapter 2), we also need a new morality.

This chapter will orbit around two Nietzschean works dealing with morality and meaning: *Beyond Good and Evil* (1886) and *On the Genealogy of Morals* (1887). Depending on the book publisher, *Genealogy of Morals* often carries the subtitle: "By way of clarification and supplement to my last book *Beyond Good and Evil.*" Hence, Nietzsche saw *Genealogy of Morals* as a concise and clarifying summation of *Beyond Good and Evil.* After highlighting some major themes in these two works, I will explain how a theology of the fall already delivered notions of *décadence*, decay, and death. Even though Nietzsche critiques Christian morality

---

a literary movement characterized by a taste for the 'gothic', a fin de siècle obsession with decay, deviance, and death." See Young, *Friedrich Nietzsche: A Philosophical Biography* (Cambridge University Press, 2010), 493.

[2] Young, *Friedrich Nietzsche*, 493.

[3] Maybe I have ingested so much of Nietzsche for over a decade that I wrote this sentence before rereading his *On the Genealogy of Morals*, and I laughed to myself when I saw in his foreword an almost identical sentence: "For me, what was at stake was the *value* of morality." See Nietzsche, *On the Genealogy of Morals: A Polemic*, trans. Douglas Smith (Oxford University Press, 1996), 7.

in *Genealogy of Moral* and *Beyond Good and Evil*, he parodies the fall to proclaim a more novel moral system.

Nietzsche's Critiques of Christian Morality

Even though one may find some lighthearted critiques of Christianity in Nietzsche's early writings,[4] the harsh criticisms are unabashedly clear in his 1880's publications. To reiterate, God is dead, metaphysics is dead, and ontology is dead, which means that morality must next die. In his preface to *On the Genealogy of Morals*, he writes:

> We stand in need of a *critique* of moral values, *the value of these values itself should first of all be called into question.* This requires a knowledge of the conditions and circumstances of their growth, development, and displacement (morality as consequence, symptom, mark, Tartufferie, illness, misunderstanding: but also morality as cause, cure, stimulant, inhibition, poison) . . . The *value* of these 'values' was accepted as given, as fact, as beyond all question. Previously, no one had expressed even the remotest doubt or shown the slightest hesitation in assuming the 'good man' to be of greater worth than the 'evil man', of greater worth in the sense of his usefulness in promoting

[4] *The Birth of Tragedy* (first published in 1872) does not offer overt or explicit criticisms against Christianity. They are certainly more subtle. Yet, in the last revised preface (1886) to *The Birth of Tragedy*, Nietzsche notes how his criticism was developing and maturing since the first publication of that early work. See Nietzsche, *The Birth of Tragedy: Out of the Spirit of Music*, trans. Shawn Whiteside, ed. Michael Tanner (Penguin, 1994).

> the progress of human *existence* (including the future of man). What? And if the opposite were the case?[5]

We might consider this statement as Nietzsche's "purpose statement" for *Genealogy of Morals*. As a purpose statement, Nietzsche clearly declares the essence of his work, which is to critique the value of values. In other words, in *Genealogy of Morals*, Nietzsche attempts to both annunciate and denunciate Western morality; he is explaining how we have naively received our current moral systems in order to then expose them as power plays that ultimately lead to death and *décadence*. However, before delving into some of his specific critiques (mainly) against Christianity, we need to further exegete his purpose statement.

First, what is a critique of the value of values? His main attention is on *Christian* values, which is to say, a Christian morality. Now, to critique the value of Christian values is to develop a *meta*-analysis of a topic. We could even say that Nietzsche is dealing with the discipline of **metaethics**, which examines philosophical foundations of morality, such as exploring certain underlying assumptions and justifications for moral beliefs and actions. To ask the question, "What is the value of value?" is to ask a meta-ethical question. Nietzsche desires to know what Europeans mean by "good" and "bad" by tracing their genealogical history and development. Noting these phenomena among Americans (and Westerners broadly) in our present day, Alasdair MacIntyre writes:

> [The person's] dilemma . . . is whether to act as her judgments about how it is best to act dictate or as her strong

[5] Nietzsche, *Genealogy of Morals*, 8.

> desires dictate. How, she will now ask, did I come to have the judgments that I do? What makes them genuinely mine? . . . What through that narrative she may become able to ask is whether and how far she identifies with her judgments, whether and how far she identifies with her desires.[6]

Westerners seem to assume that certain persons, actions, beliefs, and behaviors are "good/bad," but why and on what grounds have they been making such assumptions? Nothing should be taken for granted, so Christian morality—the ethical foundation of Western culture—must be called into question.

Second, in his purpose statement, Nietzsche begins to hint at what Christian morality is: It is a symptom, an illness, a cause, a stimulant, an inhibition, a poison. Nietzsche's medical metaphors are intentional. Each of these words reveals Nietzsche's stance on Christian morality as a noxious system poisoning the European masses to death. Existentially and socially, they are slowly dying from a morality that promises "life," and that's the epitome of a toxic and decadent morality, according to Nietzsche—something that promises life but in the end delivers death. Yet, what specifically makes Christian morality deathly?

Anthropology (what it means to be human) and morality (how human beings should live) are inseparable. It is in and through our bodies that we live, move, and have our being as moral agents. As developed in the last chapter, Nietzsche attempted to upend Greek and Christian forms of anthropology

---

[6] Alasdair MacIntyre, *Ethics in the Conflicts of Modernity: An Essay on Desire, Practical Reason, and Desire* (Cambridge University Press, 2016), 43.

to reimagine a new frontier for humanity: the human *becoming*. Although some Enlightenment-era figures tried to unweave the Christian concept of the human being, it was Nietzsche who cut the thread completely, and to erect a new morality, Nietzsche needed to launch a strong attack on Christian morality to finally bury it. In order to do this well, he recognized that Europeans needed fresh moral categories to describe themselves as they learned to navigate new social horizons. Let's explore some of those Nietzschean moral categories.

First we have *ressentiment*. Like the French word *décadence*, Nietzsche adopts and adapts this French word for his philosophical aims. This term is more emotional than it is conceptual or rational for Nietzsche. *Ressentiment* is the "emotion of legitimacy" of slave moralities.[7] According to Nietzsche, *ressentiment* began when slaves (primarily Jews) reacted to the noble classes oppressing and dominating them: "The pathos of nobility and distance, the enduring, dominating, and fundamental overall feeling of a higher ruling kind in relation to a lower kind, to a 'below'—*that* is the origin of the opposition between 'good' and 'bad.'"[8] Thus, morality has an origin, an ethical "big bang."

But, before we can arrive at this origin, we must understand the conditions that catalyzed the beginning of these traditional categories of "good" and "bad." These conditions, says Nietzsche, spawned because of a social tension between two classes: masters and slaves.[9] Historically, Nietzsche claims, the slave class seems

---

[7] Robert C. Solomon, "One Hundred Years of Ressentiment: Nietzsche's Genealogy of Morals," in *Nietzsche, Genealogy, Morality: Essays on Nietzsche's "Genealogy of Morals,"* ed. Richard Schacht (University of California Press, 1994), 124.

[8] Nietzsche, *Genealogy of Morals*, 13.

[9] Nietzsche, *Genealogy of Morals*, 19.

to be rooted in the Israelites and their sensibility against elites and nobles.[10] Seeing their conditions in Egypt, the Hebrews became angry and hostile, thereby overthrowing Pharaoh and the Egyptians, and that's not the end of the psychological story for Nietzsche. The Jews cannot let go of their *ressentiment*; instead, they internalize it, weaponize it, and become vindictive. As he writes, "Priests [Jews] are, as is well-known, the *most evil* enemies—but why? Because they are the most powerless. From powerlessness their hatred grows to take on a monstrous and sinister shape."[11]

Nietzsche admits that such an emotional vindictiveness did not historically spread overnight: "It is a long time before this instinct dominates to such an extent that the moral value-judgment catches and sticks fast on this opposition."[12] Eventually, the herd instinct of *ressentiment* was spread among the European "plebians" (commoners), infiltrating their societies and cultures through the spreading of the poisonous values and ideals of "good," "bad," "salvation," "weakness," and "love."[13] This included Jewish and Christian believers, who used resentment—bitterness, hostility, hatred, anger, malice—against others as a weapon to influence or, perhaps better, infect societies. This *ressentiment*, according to Nietzsche, over time conditioned European culture to value what slave and herd moralities call "good" and "bad." In sum, Nietzsche here is trying to develop a psychosociological reading of morality.[14] He's tracing its genealogy, including

---

[10] See Nietzsche, *Genealogy of Morals*, 19–21.

[11] Nietzsche, *Genealogy of Morals*, 19.

[12] Nietzsche, *Genealogy of Morals*, 13.

[13] Nietzsche, *Genealogy of Morals*, 21.

[14] We could even add a philological reading of morality. For instance, Nietzsche constantly flexes his philological training by

its developments within various societies, in order to discover its origins, so the European populace can finally see the world unmasked. According to Nietzsche, there's an order of operations to the *décadence* he's witnessing in his day. The creation of morality begins with a type of class struggle between the aristocratic master and the slave or herdsman, which then instigates an emotional posture within the latter group. This emotional posture then conditions a vitriolic vindictiveness against the aristocracy, developing *ressentiment*. This *ressentiment* catalyzes a kind of morality that labels the master as "bad" and the slave as "good," shaming the aristocratic master and elevating the slave into moral power.

The next two important moral terms for Nietzsche are *denial* and *depreciation*. Nietzsche criticizes both Platonism and Christianity for prioritizing the spiritual realm (the transcendent) and unattainable ideals over the tangible world (the immanent) and the present moment. Platonism and Christianity were too otherworldly and thus depreciated earthly, tangible realities. Christian morality, for instance, seems to be focused on ethereality, spiritual intangibles, and souls, thus repressing, denying, and disregarding physical, earthly life. This is one of the reasons why he refers to Christian morals as *décadent*.

"Life itself," writes Nietzsche, "is to my mind the instinct for growth, for durability, for an accumulation of forces, for *power*:

---

connecting numerous etymologies in *Genealogy of Morals*. It is difficult to cite where he demonstrates this because he does it so often. Hence, a cursory reading of *On the Genealogy of Morals* reveals how evident this is. So, we might say rather humorously that Nietzsche practices a psycho-sociophilological hermeneutic of morality in both *On the Genealogy of Morals* and *Beyond Good and Evil*.

where the will to power is lacking there is decline."[15] Similar to the conclusion made in the last chapter, Nietzsche insists that to be fully alive is to exert a will to power over the Other because to do so is to be psychologically aligned with the biological and cosmological wills to power. Bruce Ellis Benson explains, "At root, décadence is simply being against life. And, since instincts (which are for Nietzsche, inherently concerned with the *self*) are the expression of life, being against them is equivalent to being against life."[16] Tying it to the present discussion on morality, Nietzsche asserts that being alive is to exert one's will to power, and in so doing he participates in self-actualizing life that fights against *décadant* living that enslaves and obstructs the will to power.

As a philosopher of his age, Nietzsche echoes other notable figures—both European and American—who articulated a morality based on natural states of life. For instance, Ralph Waldo Emerson—whom Nietzsche read and *greatly* admired[17]—believed conformity to traditional moralities as immoral living, whereas self-reliance and self-creation (read: will to power) were the pathways to true virtuous living.[18] Additionally and similar to Emerson's attendance to nature, Nietzsche exalted natural, primitive, and native states because that's where power and force can be found in their most pure forms. Thus, Nietzsche critiqued Christian morality because of its attempts to control and tame

---

[15] Quote from Hollingdale's translation of Nietzsche, *Anti-Christ*, 6.

[16] Bruce Ellis Benson, *Pious Nietzsche: Decadence and Dionysian Faith* (Indiana University Press, 2008), 58.

[17] On this relationship, see Hermann Hummel, "Emerson and Nietzsche," *New England Quarterly*. 19.1 (1946): 63–84.

[18] *The Collected Works of Ralph Waldo Emerson*, ed. Robert Spiller et al. (Harvard University Press, 1971), 2:32.

the sensual and natural—the will to power—and "convert" the animality within us.[19]

Écrasez l'inflâme and the Future of Morality

Building upon the last section, I will now couple Nietzsche's criticism of Christian morality within his philosophical arc (especially in the 1880s) that expected new future horizons of moral possibility. In this section, I will interweave important portions of the first two chapters to make explicit connections between Nietzsche's overarching philosophical goals and his expected new moral order.

Greco-Christianized ideas reveal discreditable symptoms for Nietzsche, and any symptom assumes "causes." Yet, Nietzsche doesn't choose the "scientific" jargon of cause-and-effect, because in doing so it borrows from certain Aristotelian and Enlightenment categories, the same ones he is attempting to transcend. Thus, after an evaluation of various idol-like norms in Western societies, he diagnoses these cultural symptoms as stemming from a *force*, because forces, not causes, *connote power and dominion*. This reflects some of the observations made in the previous chapters. For starters, one of Nietzsche's goals was to expose not what ideologies are but *whose* they are.[20] As we

---

[19] On this topic, Nietzsche writes, "Mankind continues to suffer from the after-effects of these naïve priestly cures! . . . With the priests, *everything* becomes more dangerous, not only cures and therapies, but also arrogance, revenge, perspicacity, extravagance, love, the desire to dominate, virtue, illness." See Nietzsche, *Genealogy of Morals*, 18.

[20] For Nietzsche and for postmodernists like Deleuze, all reality is interpretation, which has some warrant. Yet, Deleuze takes this interpretive principle a step further: "We see that the art of interpreting

noted in the last chapter about ontology, Nietzsche understood "being" as a bankrupt concept because of its origin in the Greek-Christian narrative. Hence, the need for a better ontology without the bondages of prior systems. The path forward, according to Nietzsche, is to unveil the powerful forces creating social tensions *through* those Greek-Christian ideas and ideologies.

In Nietzsche's schema, the world is filled with a multitude of forces relationally conflicting and warring with one another. French philosopher Gilles Deleuze clarifies Nietzsche's understanding of force along these lines: "We will never find the sense of something (of a human, a biological or even a physical phenomenon) if we do not know the force which appropriates the thing, which exploits it, which takes possession of it or is expressed in it. . . . All force is appropriation, domination, exploitation of a quantity of reality."[21] Contrasting himself with the language of Western (and Christian) philosophy, Nietzsche offers new paradigms of how we think about and live in society. "Cause" is translated to "force," and "effect" is translated as "symptom." Behind every *thing* is an appropriation of force or power. As Deleuze puts it, "The history of a thing . . . is the succession of forces which take possession of it and the co-existence of the forces which struggle for possession."[22] Granted, we're reading Nietzsche through the lens of Deleuze, yet, as I see it, Deleuze is carefully expositing the German philosopher. To know a thing, then, is to know *whose* it is and how it is being used.

---

must also be an art of piercing masks, of discovering the one that masks himself, why he does it and the point of keeping up the mask while it is being reshaped." See Gilles Deleuze, *Nietzsche and Philosophy*, trans. Hugh Tomlinson (Columbia University Press, 1983), 5.

[21] Deleuze, *Nietzsche and Philosophy*, 3.

[22] Deleuze, *Nietzsche and Philosophy*, 3.

Looking back again to the preface of his *Genealogy of Morals*, Nietzsche states that every culture has an indeterminate number of values, and these values are connected to forces in competition. It is the genealogist's job to discover these forces at work and to unmask them. For Nietzsche, a genealogical reading of any topic, like morality, was not merely a descriptive, historical exploration; genealogies function as historical critiques intended to overthrow cultural norms by exposing their evangelists as hypocrites and their ideas as idols. For the German philosopher, genealogical readings functioned apocalyptically because they exposed how power *always already* influenced "truth."[23]

In *Beyond Good and Evil*, Nietzsche wants to transcend (hence, the preposition "beyond" in *Beyond Good and Evil*) the current theological and philosophical categories we have accepted as gospel truth. He maintains that we must rise and will ourselves into this unexplored and indigenous metaphysic and morality. In fact, he goes as far as to claim that the (European) world cries out for a messiah—also referred to as an overman (*Übermensch*)—who can attain such a vision and recreate society so that it will fearlessly and courageously follow and help erect this brave new world. The *Übermensch* is the one who overcomes the hypocrisy and idolatry; he is the one who exercises the will to power (more on this in chapter 6).

As surveyed in the last chapter, that which is organic, natural, or instinctual is the will to power, and to repress this will to power is to participate in the old world order with its restraints,

---

[23] For a fuller exposition of Nietzsche's genealogical method, see Michel Foucault, "Nietzsche, Genealogy, History" in *Language, Counter-Memory, and Practice: Selected Essays and Interviews*, ed. D. F. Bouchard (Cornell University Press, 1977).

oppressions, and domineering of persons. In the Nietzschean framework, the *Übermensch* is the true genealogist because he can unveil ideas as idols and reveal societal symptoms with its underlying forces. Nietzsche's *Übermensch* looks backward as much as he does forward; he retrieves a **Dionysian** state while ushering in this future eschatological society. In Greek tragedies, Dionysus subverted oppressive restraints by leading his believers into a freedom of festive play, including drinking and dance. Dionysus was known "as a god who licensed free speech, satire and an aggressive, sometimes 'consequential' mockery of individuals."[24]

However, for Nietzsche, Dionysus was more than a Greek god. Dionysus functions for Nietzsche as a philosophical psyche or even a way of being, such that one should seek to have their life possessed by a Dionysian spirit, reorienting the person into a liberated life. Neither social nor ethical norms ever repressed Dionysus, because the "Dionysian is that which transcends concepts."[25] A Dionysian, as Young illustrates, is one who is intoxicated "or, better, [in a state of] 'ecstasy', a standing out of oneself [*ex-stasis*], out of everyday consciousness."[26] Simply put, the Dionysian overcomes that which binds. To frame it within a Kantian schema, there exist appearances (phenomena) and true realities (noumena), and Kant suspected we can, at best, only perceive appearances and not realities in themselves.[27] In contrast, Nietzsche asserts that he has found a way out of the world

---

[24] Eric Csapo, "The 'Theology' of the Dionysia and Old Comedy," in *Theologies of Ancient Greek Religion*, ed. Esther Eidenow, Julia Kindt, and Robin Osborne (Cambridge University Press, 2016), 118.

[25] Young, *Friedrich Nietzsche*, 128.

[26] Young, *Friedrich Nietzsche*, 127.

[27] Here is another reminder to glance back at the outline in chapter 1 of Nietzsche's historical epochs.

of appearances, and Dionysus has given him the cup of salvation. Through a Dionysian aesthetic, a sublime experience (often through music) ushers us into ecstasy and a transcendence above all worldly, phenomenal appearances.

Nietzsche's figure of Zarathustra is a true Dionysian, because he testifies against Platonic-Christian *décadence* and valuelessness.[28] The Dionysian exercises the will to power over the criminality of the former five epochs of philosophy (see the epochal chart from chapter 1). For Nietzsche, a new destiny is dawning where the old concepts, with their enslaving metaphysics and morality, are being exceeded. Nietzsche names several terms affiliated with Christianity that have enslaved European societies since their beginnings: God, hereafter, true world, soul, spirit, immortal soul, holy, salvation of the soul, sin, free will, selfless, self-denying, duty, holiness, divinity, and good. Each of these terms, says Nietzsche, have destroyed, poisoned, deformed, slandered, and misshapen all Western societies.[29] In order to inaugurate the future world, we must leave behind this former one by crushing it.

As a battle cry to those who have ears to hear, Nietzsche chants in the closing of *Ecce Homo* the words *Écrasez l'inflâme!* "Crush the infamy!" The term *l'inflâme* could also be translated "monster," as Voltaire intended it.[30] This motto Nietzsche borrows from Voltaire in his battle against all religions, especially Christianity, that attempted to subdue and silence people. The

---

[28] In the conclusion of *Ecce Homo,* Nietzsche consistently interchanges Zarathustra with Dionysus. See Nietzsche, *Ecce Homo: How to Become What You Are*, trans. Duncan Large (Oxford University Press, 2009), 94–95.

[29] See Nietzsche, *Ecce Homo*, 95.

[30] James Parton, *Life of Voltaire* (Houghton Mifflin, 1881), 2:653.

only way forward for Nietzsche is to now arm the brigades. To commence the beginning of the end, the metanarratives, metaphysics, and morality of Plato and Christianity must be fully annihilated.

The Fall: Forbidden Fruits, *Décadence*, Decay, and Death

Shortly after the creation of the cosmic order with its Milky Way, mushrooms, and mankind, the story takes a quick downturn. After fashioning humanity, God delivers them a divinely empowered mandate to "be fruitful, multiply, fill the earth" and additionally to "subdue" his created order by tending to it and cultivating it (Gen 1:28; cf. 2:15). And just like any good story, the suspense builds into conflict: Humanity is charmed by a temptuous, cunning creature who asks, "Did God really say, 'You can't eat from any tree in the garden'?" To this the humans reply, "We may eat the fruit from the trees in the garden. But about the fruit of the tree in the middle of the garden, God said, 'You must not eat it or touch it, or you will die.'" (3:2–3). The tempter's response is worth quoting in full:

> "No! You will certainly not die," the serpent said to the woman. "In fact, God knows that when you eat it your eyes will be opened and you will be like God, knowing good and evil." The woman saw that the tree was good for food and delightful to look at, and that it was desirable for obtaining wisdom. So she took some of its fruit and ate it; she also gave some to her husband, who was with her, and he ate it. Then the eyes of both of them were opened, and they knew they were naked; so they

> sewed fig leaves together and made coverings for themselves (3:4–7).

This event, often referred to as "the fall," marks a seismic shift in three relationships: the one between God and humanity, the one between humanity and humanity, and the one between humanity and creation. Previously existing in a state of deep connection and communion, human beings, as a consequence of their disobedience, inaugurate death and decay into the world, affecting a multitude of relationships (3:14–19). To an extent then, we must agree with Nietzsche: *Décadence* is not only evidential but also very existential. But before we explore the consequences of decay and death after the fall, I want to briefly sketch how Nietzsche parodies the categories of Genesis 3 concerning morality.

As outlined earlier in this chapter, Nietzsche believed that the invention of morality commences because of a class struggle between master and slave, specifically between the Jews and their foreign oppressor. Through this struggle, an internal response erupts within the slave psyche, thereby hating the master and developing a social discord and disharmony. Growing from within this tension is the invention of and a "knowing [of] good and evil." Slowly but surely, through a series of massive slave revolts over centuries, slaves then transvaluated values that were eventually inherited by European culture,[31] a notion Nietzsche calls the "bad conscience."[32] According to Nietzsche, this psychological development became ingrained in the human conscience and caused it to be absorbed with guilt, credit, and shame,

---

[31] Nietzsche, *Genealogy of Morals*, 19–20.

[32] Nietzsche, *Genealogy of Morals*, 68.

thereby poisoning Europe for centuries.[33] The primary instigator of this guilt, states Nietzsche, is the Christian faith. Despite the decline of faith in the Christian God, Nietzsche notes, one would think that the "human sense of guilt should have weakened considerably."[34] But the European world continues to live in its shadows; hence the need for and expectation of the Great Noon and the transvaluation of traditional morals and values.

This brief synopsis does not do full justice to Nietzsche's development of his argument throughout *Genealogy of Morals*, yet I do believe it's a fair and approximate summation. I offer this outline to demonstrate two main points. First, through his genealogical method, Nietzsche insists that we must eat from *his* psychological and philosophical forbidden fruit to know the true and real *origins* of good and evil.[35] Like the enemy in the primordial garden, Nietzsche entices us with a knowledge of how things *really* are, such as the origination of "good" and "bad," the cultural development of these terms throughout Western history,

---

[33] Nietzsche, *Genealogy of Morals*, 72–76.

[34] Nietzsche, *Genealogy of Morals*, 71.

[35] Directly engaging this topic in his work, Stephen Mulhall also captures Nietzsche's conundrum: "For Nietzsche that profoundly determinative human perversion of the human is to be found in our acceptance of the Christian myth of the Fall; that is, our acceptance of the doctrine of human nature as Fallen is itself the moment of our true Fall, a falling away from celebrating natural nobility and life itself and turning toward a reactive condemnation of nobility and life as evil." See Mulhall, *Philosophical Myths of the Fall* (Princeton University Press, 2005), 38. In other words, as Nietzsche tries to liberate himself and Europe from Christian myths like the fall, he introduces his own notions of what it means to be fallen. Hence, this is another example of Nietzsche parodying of the biblical-theological arc of Scripture for his own purposes.

and even a taste of true (Nietzschean) enlightenment as we lean into the future.[36]

Second, Nietzsche underscores that Europe's Christianized moral culture is poisonous, deathly, horrific, myopic, sick, *décadent*, and a long string of other colorful metaphors. Remember that *Genealogy of Morals* and *Beyond Good and Evil* have a philosophical aim of transitioning Europe *beyond* its traditional morals and values. So, what is beyond on the moral horizon? Again, to "know good and evil" as Nietzsche presents them, we must wrestle with the possibility of a new existence established by new morals and values. Unfortunately, Nietzsche does not realize how deeply dependent he is upon Christian metaphors and meanings in his writings. The story of the fall, in part, reveals humanity's deepest wants and desires: to be like God. The devil is in the details though. Humanity was already fashioned in the image and likeness of God to be *like* him (Gen 1:26–28), yet the serpent's cunningness seems to imply, "Don't you want *to be* God?" Nietzsche steals from and adapts this scene to ask similarly, "Does it make sense to conceive of a god 'beyond good and evil'?"[37] In other words, Nietzsche cunningly encourages humanity to stop eating from all the other trees in the garden of Christian morality to taste the forbidden Nietzschean fruit of a new moral world order. Maybe, just maybe, we can move beyond this Christian God, with his moral *décadence*, into unknown horizons beyond Eden. For Nietzsche, Europe needs new moral

---

[36] In fact, Nietzsche believed that philosophers should be the ones leading the way: A philosopher's "'knowing' is *creating*, their creating is a law-giving, their will to truth is—*will to power*." See Nietzsche, *Beyond Good and Evil*, 122.

[37] Nietzsche, *The Will to Power*, trans. Walter Kaufmann and R. J. Hollingdale (Vintage, 1968), 55.

order—a grand reversal of morality—but "who is strong enough to undertake it?"[38]

Nietzsche's Morality in the Modern Cultural Imagination

As noted in the introductory chapter, several cultures, communities, organizations, individuals, and so on have reappropriated Nietzsche for their own purposes over the last century and a quarter. To this point, Alasdair MacIntyre considers Nietzsche to be *the* moral philosopher of our day.[39] Consistently, we discover within Western culture a fascination with Nietzsche's call to a new morality. Whether such Westernized individuals have read Nietzsche or not, they have certainly been inspirited by his *Geist* to heed the call to go beyond Christian moral concepts of "good" and "evil." Almost like a general leading his army of soldiers into cultural battle, Nietzsche heralded: "Once your ship has strayed onto this course: well then! All right! Grit your teeth bravely! Open your eyes! Keep your hand at the helm!—we are going to be travelling *beyond* morality, and by daring to travel there we may in the process stifle or crush whatever remnant of morality we have left—but what do *we* matter!"[40] According to Nietzsche's schema, "God, man, and nature were thus devoid of sense and meaning. There was no ultimate purposes and no transcendent guidance or goals for human beings."[41] In response,

[38] Nietzsche, *Genealogy of Morals*, 75.

[39] Alasdair MacIntyre, *After Virtue: A Study in Moral Theory*, 2nd ed. (Duckworth, 1985), 107.

[40] Nietzsche, *Beyond Good and Evil*, 24.

[41] Michael Allen Gillespie, *Nietzsche's Final Teaching* (University of Chicago Press, 2017), 18.

many Westerners, especially Americans, have attempted to heed this call to demonstrate they are "strong enough to undertake it" by experimenting with new meanings and moral topographies.

Speaking about this open-ended spiritual morality, Bruce Benson rightly notes, "I think that Nietzsche would say that he 'believes that he believes' not, of course, in the God of Christianity but in the god of his Dionysian Piety. . . . But, of course, Dionysus has always been the god of masks, change and metamorphosis, and deception."[42] In other words, Nietzsche's Dionysus had to die a thousand deaths, over and over, to operate with new faces and new possibilities.

As outlined in chapter 1, Nietzsche anticipates a future world without the Christian God, yet he foresees fresh forms of god(s) with accompanying spiritualities. To use a modern term, we might call these gods and spiritualties "mysticisms." As Andrew Root charts in *The Church in an Age of Secular Mysticisms*, these mysticisms have been drastically on the rise from the twentieth century onward. Mysticism "arose without any need or concern for God. This mysticism without God could arrive because guilt returned. This guilt did not come from a divine command, with eternal consequence or practices of forgiveness. Instead, this guilt came about because of the demand to make the self into something magnificent (hence the escalation of self-help, self-development, and self-esteem movements and markets in the 1980s and beyond)."[43]

Modern mysticisms are secularized pieties because they attempt to discover meaning within an **immanent frame** without

---

[42] Benson, *Pious Nietzsche*, 190.

[43] Andrew Root, *The Church in an Age of Secular Mysticisms: Why Spiritualities Without God Fail to Transform Us* (Baker Academic, 2023), 64.

(former) theologies, metaphysics, or moral norms. As Root says, moral guilt is no longer connected to divine otherness or transcendent holiness. In other words, guilt does not come from external forces; it has been transvalued. It is internalized and situated within the self who serves as both judge and justifier. As Root frames it, "The most harsh judgments of the self are aimed at the self. The self is so cruel that there is often no route to restoration and forgiveness. It becomes hard—an overwhelming life task—for late-modern people to learn strategies to forgive themselves (always by themselves)."[44] This is one way (among many) Nietzsche's vision of morality has been appropriated and imbibed in the modern cultural imagination.

In conclusion, Nietzsche invited European culture to experience a (Dionysian) metamorphosis and to drink of his moral wines that generate a nontraditional, self-actualizing life. For Nietzsche, that's how Europe must fight the *décadant* Christian morality. The self for Nietzsche becomes the site of a groundbreaking and unexplored morality. The body trailblazes a new value of values, opening infinite horizons for moral opportunities. Ironically, Nietzsche's moral opportunities are nothing more than masked, secularized pieties that cannot escape the immanent frame because God is dead.[45] These pieties long for an absolution of moral guilt and shame without a loving and forgiving God. As demonstrated, Nietzsche's philosophical hopes were not novel. He parodies the fall by accidentally playing the part of the serpent who promises true knowledge and godlikeness

[44] Root, *The Church in an Age of Secular Mysticisms*, 65.

[45] Root even points out how both Edmund Husserl and Nietzsche both attempted to escape the "deadening flatness" of everyday life. See Root, *Secular Mysticisms*, 68.

while instigating death, decay, and *décadance* into all relational spheres.[46] In the end, Nietzsche's future morality overpromises what it cannot deliver, much like the serpent's promises to Adam and Eve.

The Hospitable Church: Learning How to Become Good

Speaking about twentieth-century art (but with implications going beyond the artistic community), Charles Taylor writes, "Twentieth-century art has gone more inward, has tended to explore, even to celebrate subjectivity; it has explored new recesses of feeling, entered the stream of consciousness, spawned schools of art rightly called 'expressionist.'"[47] This turn inward and the individualizing of morality and values has unpredictably birthed an age of hypersensitivity and cultural outrage.

For instance, Nietzsche's moral system much more frequently appeals to *pathos* (emotion) rather than *ethos* (authority or character) or *logos* (logic or reason). Obviously, Nietzsche develops reasoned arguments (*logos*) for his future world, yet he intentionally crafts most of his writings using aphorisms and poetic prose as an act of defiance against the rhetoric of ancient Greek philosophers and Christian apologists for the past two millennia. He also does so in order to persuade the imaginative, emotive heart and not the reasoned mind. Thus, *logos* is not his

---

[46] The narrative of Gen 3 illustrates long before Nietzsche that anything *décadent* is against life, flourishing, and shalom. See Benson, *Pious Nietzsche*, 58.

[47] Charles Taylor, *Sources of the Self: The Making of the Modern Identity* (Harvard University Press, 1989), 456.

preferred rhetorical method. Also, rarely does he appeal to his character or trustworthiness (*ethos*).[48] Instead, Nietzsche wants to persuade readers with *pathos*, an emotional appeal to "feel" the European world a certain way. Undoubtedly, Nietzsche desires for Europeans to be angry at the way things have become in order to stir them toward heroic action. This Nietzschean *pathos* has infiltrated an American modern imagination by marrying together subjective morals with outrage toward traditional Greco-Christian values that oppress, dismiss, violate, and marginalize. This *pathos* generates a type of "internalized oppression."

Özlem Sensoy and Robin DiAngelo define internalized oppression as "believing in and acting out (often unawarely) the constant messages circulating in the culture that you and your group are inferior to whichever group is dominant in relation to yours and that you are deserving of your lower position."[49] According to this model, recognizing one's supposed inferiority is the first step toward outrage, which develops into a type of cultural action—whether those actions be violent or peaceful. Regardless, "outrage is a safe way . . . to test whether the stage is ready for their performance. Outrage is the way to clear the stage from what you perceive to be unwelcoming. Not necessarily unwelcoming to your personhood or humanity, but to the anxious performance you need to secure your self's magnificence."[50]

---

[48] A few chapters in *Ecce Homo* are titled, "Why I Am So Wise" and "Why I Am So Clever," yet these are not *ethos*-esque appeals. Rather, *Ecce Homo* is a satirical writing meant to persuasively entertain the reader into the comedies of European *décadence*.

[49] Özlem Sensoy and Robin DiAngelo, *Is Everyone Really Equal? An Introduction to Key Concepts in Social Justice Education*, 2nd ed. (Teachers College, 2017), 44.

[50] Root, *Secular Mysticisms*, 32.

This angered *pathos* births a set of self-created expressions and values meant to rebel against certain domineering cultural narratives. More concisely, *pathos* precedes and provokes performance. And it is this outraged *pathos* that incites protest, creating social unrest by enflaming further irritation and outrage. Regretfully, this type of *pathos* rarely seeks social solutions or shalom. One of its aims is to curb attitudes and dispositions to see the world negatively and angrily, thereby not catalyzing concrete justice and hope.

To reiterate, when we locate this *pathos* within the Western social imagination, many Americans inherit varieties of Nietzsche's disdain, outrage, and anger against Christianity. This Nietzschean emotion has seeped into the American modern mindset, where rejection of Christian values ripens into subjective moralities and self-discovered performances. So, if Americans have imbibed this Nietzschean *pathos*, then how can the church learn how to become good in an age that celebrates expressivist individualism and subjectivity? The phrase "learning how to become good" may be off-putting to some of you. In the larger context of this phrase, I simply mean, "What does embodying of the gospel look like in a culture persuaded by this Nietzschean *pathos*?"

This angered *pathos* is not always easy to see within culture. In fact, I want to briefly elucidate a cultural symptom of this internalized *pathos*, a symptom in the American church that sociologists call "dechurching." The term dechurched refers to individuals who were once part of a church but have since left or become disconnected from it. In their book *The Great Dechurching*, Jim Davis and Michael Graham furnish several nuanced reasons why individuals leave churches, yet there are threads of consistent themes: "The list of these points of trauma and frustration is long, but it includes spiritual and physical abuse in the church, hypocrisy among church members and leaders, sexual ethics, political syncretism, political disagreement, suffering, racism, bigotry, and a perceived lack of relevance or real answers to the world's problems."[51] Again, this notion of dechurching is best described as a collection of symptoms with imbedded causes, rooted (among many influences) in a Nietzschean-influenced *pathos*. To clarify, notice the list provided by Davis and Graham in the quote above. Each reason (right or wrong) for dechurching is stimulated by an emotional unrest, a kind of *ressentiment*, with churches.[52] The modern cultural imagination, following Nietzsche, has concluded that Christians (and by extension, churches) do not provide "real answers to the world's problems."This disappointment ferments new possibilities of how to navigate their world without God, religion, and traditional ethical norms. Such a groping for discovery, as Root mentioned earlier, paves the way for an "anxious performance . . . to secure your self's magnificence," thus creating novel individualized pieties and spiritualities.[53] On deeper inspection, this emotional unrest reveals a longing for a remedy

---

[51] Jim Davis and Michael Graham, *The Great Dechurching: Who's Leaving, Why Are They Going, and What Will It Take to Bring Them Back?* (Zondervan, 2023), 24.

[52] See the discussion on *ressentiment* toward the beginning of this chapter. As a reminder, *ressentiment*, according to Nietzsche, begins with conflict between a slave and noble class, generating a *pathos* of hostility. Ironically, Nietzsche interprets *ressentiment* as the origin of the concepts of "good" and "bad," yet he perpetuates this *ressentiment* of conflict and hostility through his outrage.

[53] Root, *Secular Mysticisms*, 32.

and solution, which Davis and Graham reveal is a possibility for the dechurched: "When we focused on why this group of people left the church and how they thought they would come back, the answer was simple: belonging."[54]

Even as the dechurched leave God, religion, and former ethical norms, they still carry guilt and shame, hence the longing for resolution and absolution. Your dechurched neighbor searches for hope in and through cultural philosophies, practices, narratives, and ideologies ultimately rooted in the heroic self. As Davis and Graham illustrate, such individuals would consider revisiting faith communities, but this return would require a resonating sense of belonging. Thankfully, Scripture already narrates a framework for cultivating spaces of belonging through the practice of hospitality.

Hospitality was personified in the person of Jesus, and because it was embodied in him, the practice of hospitality was interwoven into the ethical activity of the early church. For example, Paul writes these words to the church at Rome: "Be devoted to one another in brotherly love; . . . contributing to the needs of the saints, practicing hospitality" (Rom 12:10, 13, NASB). Sylvia C. Keesmaat and Brian J. Walsh explain that Roman social relations were known for exploitation, control, suspicion, and violence; thus, hospitable embrace of non-Romans or lesser classes (women, plebeians, slaves, freedpersons) by Romans was *not* the ethical custom:

> This vision of economic graciousness and love [in Romans 12] is reinforced by Paul's language of debt in Romans 1:14. Recall that Paul says that he is indebted

[54] Davis and Graham, *Great Dechurching*, 27.

> to both Greeks and barbarians, to both wise and foolish. One could hardly imagine a more striking reversal of imperial notions of debt. In Paul's understanding, those who are clearly at the despised and shamed bottom of the imperial hierarchy of honor and debt are elevated to the same level as those at the top of the cultural system.[55]

As a matter of application of Paul's call for radical hospitality in Rom 12, the church can embrace dechurched neighbors whose guilt, shame, and anxiety have dissociated them from fellowship. Those who carry the labels of being despised, shamed, and forgotten by the church can discover embrace, *if* the church recaptures this scriptural vision and practice of hospitality. In conclusion, the love, mercy, and forgiveness of Jesus can extinguish this moral *pathos* of guilt and shame while removing the social obstacles that have excluded the dechurched from a community rooted in the "very good" and meaning-full presence of the triune God.

---

[55] Sylvia C. Keesmaat and Brian J. Walsh, *Romans Disarmed: Resisting Empire, Demanding Justice* (Brazos, 2019), 237–38.

Chapter 5

Hebrew Prophets and Nietzsche's Zarathustra (On Truth)

Until this moment in the present work, you may feel conflicted with Nietzsche. For instance, you may find some resonance with Nietzsche's philosophical agenda: He was disgusted with numerous manipulations and false promises of Christianity, especially the Lutheran pietism of his day.[1] As the previous chapter showed, Nietzsche believed the Christian

[1] Stephen Williams's point is illuminating: "Although it is a mistake to interpret [Nietzsche's] anti-Christianity mainly in terms of the churches of his day, his own experience of contemporary Christianity must have played a part." Williams, *The Shadow of the Antichrist: Nietzsche's Critique of Christianity* (Baker Academic, 2006), 131. As I read Nietzsche, many of his critiques against Christianity are really attacks against the *cultural* Christianities of his day. Nietzsche did not distinguish between a robust, orthodox, and biblical Christianity and a diluted culturalization of Christianity. For a title that helpfully demonstrates how the church can be faithfully orthodox while acknowledging its cultural embeddedness, see John Webster, *The Culture of Theology* (Baker, 2019).

faith had become narrowly focused on nonphysical, intangible, and spiritual realities while disregarding concrete, tangible, and material realities. Likewise, contemporary evangelicalism is guilty of being overly spiritualizing by degrading creation and twisting salvation into a modern Neoplatonism where God is only concerned with "saving souls."[2] This obsession with only otherworldly realms, Nietzsche argued, leads to *décadence*—a degradation of life itself, a cheapening of morality, and a starving of the will to power. Nietzsche ultimately believed that *décadence* was nothing more than a form of **nihilism**.[3]

This term "nihilism" is a complex notion in Nietzsche's corpus, yet it orbits around a radical rejection of value and meaning, which was ultimately promoted by the traditional values of ancient Greek philosophy, Judaism, and Christianity. These traditional values were the chief proponents of nihilism because they, as noted in previous chapters, promoted a metaphysics and morality *against* life or against our true nature, which, for Nietzsche,

---

[2] A couple of notable works on the former topic in the past two decades include Steven Bouma-Prediger, *For the Beauty of the Earth: A Christian Vision for Creation Care* (Baker Academic, 2001), Bouma-Prediger, *Earthkeeping and Character: Exploring a Christian Ecological Virtue Ethic* (Baker Academic, 2019), Andrew J. Spencer, *Hope for God's Creation: Stewardship in an Age of Futility* (B&H Academic, 2023). For a stellar critique on the latter topic, see N. T. Wright, *Surprised by Hope: Rethinking Heaven, the Resurrection, and the Mission of the Church* (HarperOne, 2018).

[3] Michael Allen Gillespie notes: "The term 'nihilism' does not appear in [Nietzsche's] notes until 1880 or in his published work until 1886. In fact, nihilism is only one in a series of concepts that Nietzsche employed in his attempt to come to terms with the spiritual crisis of European civilization. Moreover, he used it only briefly and then abandoned it in favor of the concept of decadence." See Gillespie, *Nietzsche's Final Teaching* (University of Chicago Press, 2017), 27.

is the will to power.[4] These old traditional systems, according to Nietzsche, promoted control by regulating a person's inner will and constricting his innate power. For Nietzsche, nihilism is not merely a notion but an already but not yet reality. It is "already" because God is dead, but not yet because Nietzsche's Europe continued to live in God's shadow. In response, Nietzsche proclaims that European society needs a seer, a prophet who points to the age of post-Christendom to come.

To better understand Nietzsche's notion of nihilism and its aftermath on truth in Western society, this chapter considers the Nietzschean character Zarathustra in *Thus Spoke Zarathustra.* As we will see, Zarathustra functions as more than a fictional figure in Nietzsche's philosophical narrative; he is the prophet-like personage who signifies the future age Nietzsche longed for. After examining Zarathustra, we will (again) discover that Nietzsche's Zarathustra parodies Israel's prophets, a divinely ordained community of holy persons who prepare a people for action while longing for an imminent justice and salvation.

Nietzsche's Prophet Zarathustra

Published in 1883, Nietzsche's *Thus Spoke Zarathustra* is a fictional novel that explores the themes of individuality and the creating of personal meaning and truth. Zarathustra the prophet announces the coming of the superman (*Übermensch*), a messianic figure who announces and awakens Europe for a future society. According to Nietzsche, he is the forthcoming hope of

---

[4] For a project that unravels the lexical nuances of Nietzsche's nihilism, see Joseph Anthony Kranak, "Nietzsche's Revaluation of All Values" (PhD diss., Marquette University, 2014).

Europe because he prizes self-worth as *the* moral code to live by. He is the transvaluator of values, and in and through him the future world will be seized and inaugurated. But after his first discourse, Zarathustra realizes that no one is listening to his message, and he laments, "They understand me not: I am not the mouth for these ears." Nietzsche recognizes through Zarathustra that the society to which he preaches does not and will not understand his message because they are not ready for it. Why is this the case? It is because they cannot fathom the deaths of God, metaphysics, and the Greco-Christian morality in their age. They continue to live, move, and have their being in the shadow of God.

With near echoes of an apocalyptic scene, Nietzsche places these words on Zarathustra's tongue:

> Truly, my friends, I walk among men as among the fragments and limbs of men! The terrible thing to my eye is to find men shattered in pieces and scattered as if over a battlefield of slaughter. And when my eye flees from the present to the past, it always discovers the same thing: fragments and limbs and dreadful changes—but no men! The present and the past upon the earth—alas! my friends—that is my most intolerable burden; and I should not know how to live, if I were not a seer of what which must come.[5]

Within this scene, Nietzsche depicts Europe as nothing more than "fragments and limbs of men"—it has vestiges of humanity but no real humanity can be found. Like a "battlefield of

[5] Nietzsche, *Thus Spoke Zarathustra*, trans. R. J. Hollingdale (Penguin, 1969), 2:42.

slaughter," European society has been torn apart by the nihilism of Plato, Moses, and Jesus. Nothing of value and truth can be found in its aftermath. In fact, Western history has witnessed three metamorphoses for millennia: the spirits of the camel, the lion, and the child.

As a type of history, Nietzsche begins his discourses narrating how Europe became what it is. First, looking into its backstory, Nietzsche writes that Europe's cultural inheritance seems to begin with the spirit of the camel—a dutiful, burdensome way of life rooted in "thou shalts." This cultural stream taught the Western world to be responsible and obligated to divine dictates and universal rules. As "camels," Europe still experiences the burdening loads of universals, commandments, ordinances, statutes, and "thou shalts," prodding it into a second metamorphosis.[6]

The second spirit of the lion pushes against the spirit of the camel. Instead of promoting a life under "thou shalts," the way of the lion says, "I will." The former camel-like ways need to be nullified and buried, moving society into an irreverent rebellion against prior traditions. Society, if it desires to flourish, needs to "create new values," but "the lion is unable to do that."[7] Instead, the lion spirit pounces and seizes on former things, making a path for the third metamorphosis: the child. "The child is innocence and forgetting, a fresh start, a game, a wheel that rolls of itself, a prime movement, a holy saying of 'yes.'"[8] Nietzsche suggests that some of Europe is between the lion and the child, even though a majority is still restrained as camels. Yet, it is the child

---

[6] Nietzsche, *Thus Spake Zarathustra: A Book for All and None*, trans. Michael Hulse (Notting Hill, 2022), 19–20.

[7] Nietzsche, *Thus Spake Zarathustra*, 20.

[8] Nietzsche, *Thus Spake Zarathustra*, 20.

who commences the creation of new values and truths until the *Übermensch* arrives to model for Europe how the "self-opposing, self-overcoming will [is] intrinsic to life itself."[9]

As can be clearly seen, these three metamorphoses are representative of two understandings for Nietzsche. First, they represent a way-of-seeing and a way-of-being in the world. It's the measure of how one inhabits their present world and the future world they anticipate. Second, the three metamorphoses reflect Nietzsche's psychologizing of history and humanity. Simply put, Nietzsche perceives his metamorphoses as answering two questions, "Where are we?" and "How should we then live?" Charting what this history looks like for Nietzsche, Gillespie creates the following diagram:[10]

← HUMAN →
Great Noon
Beast   Last Man   Camel   x   Lion   Child   *Übermensch*

Commenting on this diagram, Gillespie writes:

> The death of God, and the consequent delegitimation of all divinely sanctioned commandments and moral imperatives, has brought to an end all external constraints on our passions. In the ensuing vacuum, European humanity is confronted with two possibilities, descending toward the last man or ascending toward the lion, the child, and ultimately the *Übermensch*.[11]

[9] Gillespie, *Nietzsche's Final Teaching*, 29.
[10] Gillespie, *Nietzsche's Final Teaching*, 33.
[11] Gillespie, *Nietzsche's Final Teaching*, 33.

Through the fictional character of Zarathustra, Nietzsche is announcing the necessity of these metamorphoses. If Europe truly desires a new future, it must be awakened by the prophet Zarathustra's message to take upon itself the lion spirit who can spawn such a future without the nihilistic decadence brought about by Plato, Moses, and Jesus. Nihilism is the rejection of this world and its future; it is a denial and negation of the organic, material, and biological, or as Nietzsche sometimes calls this entire worldview, a "holy 'no.'" Zarathustra's child spirit forgets Europe's nihilisms in order to willfully embrace the organic, material, and biological to reorient Europe toward affirmation, not denial, of the world. Hence, "a holy saying of 'yes.'"[12]

One final word on Zarathustra the prophet. The phrase "thus spoke Zarathustra" emulates a common prophetic formula reminiscent of the Israelite prophets in the Hebrew Bible. As a prophet, Zarathustra heralds an untimely message about the already but not yet age Europe liminally sits in. It's untimely because hearers are skeptical of its truthfulness. As Nietzsche reads history, Europe is in a "betweenness" of time, a ripe revolutionary period of what could be if she heeds the prophetic call of Zarathustra. As he proclaims, "Man is a rope, tied between beast and *Übermensch*—a rope over an abyss. . . . What is great in man is that he is a bridge and not an end: what can be loved in man is that he is going over and a going under." Helpfully summarizing Nietzsche's thoughts, Michael Gillespie writes, "Zarathustra explains to [his hearers] that just as they already in some sense are the *Übermensch*, so they are also the last man, the human who seeks mere happiness and has lost sight of anything beyond the

[12] Nietzsche, *Thus Spake Zarathustra*, 20.

momentary satisfaction of his desires."[13] If Zarathustra is correct, then he is prophesying an impending future, a realm simultaneously expiring and arriving. This already but not yet future then has ramifications for truth, among a host of other ramifications.

Nihilism and the Possibilities for Truth

As chapter 2 attempted to explain, Nietzsche had a fresh vision for the future of humanity—a type of human, an *Übermensch*, who was no longer enslaved to ancient Greek and Christian anthropologies. He envisioned this *Übermensch* as the leader of a new humanity and was convinced that Europe was nearing a tipping point within the evolutionary drama. Recognizing this cultural moment in Europe, Nietzsche writes, "We ought really to have no difficulty in seeing that when a species has arrived at its limits and is about to go over into a higher species, the goal of its evolution lies, not in the mass of its exemplars and their well-being . . . but rather in those apparently scattered and chance existences which favorable conditions have here and there produced."[14] Obviously, Nietzsche is promoting a type of evolutionary species emerging from within the human being. To become something different, a "higher species," requires new moralities and truths. But notice what Nietzsche hints at: The transition within a species does not happen "in the mass of its exemplars" but in and through "favorable conditions" in individuality that are "scattered." New moralities and truths will germinate and spread when individuals herald their own personal truths. In philosophical jargon,

[13] Gillespie, *Nietzsche's Final Teaching*, 29.

[14] Julian Young, *Friedrich Nietzsche: A Philosophical Biography* (Cambridge University Press, 2010), 197.

Nietzsche is pushing against monism or the view that there is only one true and correct view, norm, or ethic. Additionally, most descriptions of monism include the interdependence of all reality having its source in a single substance, like the Christian God or the Platonic forms. In other words, he advocates for the plurality and multiplicity of truths, thus birthing a notion called **perspectivalism**. Truth is not unitary, as it had been previously conceived in ancient Greek and Christian sources, and created things do not participate in the truth as contrived in Plato's *methexis*. For Nietzsche, truth is both pluralized and unhinged from a unifying source. Before untangling what Nietzsche means by perspectivalism, it is necessary to first situate Nietzsche's nihilism into this conversation.

Nietzsche's nihilism "involves a twofold movement—a 'devaluing' and a 'revaluing' of values."[15] In Nietzsche's mind, to offer fertile conditions for something new to grow, the old must be discarded, hence a devaluing for the sake of revaluing. Underneath Nietzsche's hope for this future reality is a type of social Darwinism.[16] In short, social Darwinism is a sociological application of Darwin's biological "survival of the fittest" where individuals can evolve into stronger species given the right conditions, but, like biological Darwinism, these metamorphoses are dependent upon random conditions. Connecting the conversation to Zarathustra, Nietzsche prophesizes that such a future humanity will inhabit a world with fresh values and truths

[15] Bruce Ellis Benson, *Graven Ideologies: Nietzsche, Derrida, and Marion on Modern Idolatry* (IVP Academic, 2008), 89.

[16] Although not an extreme Darwinian, Nietzsche certainly believed Darwin was correct in many of his observations. See Nietzsche, *Sämtliche Briefe: Kritische Studienausgabe*, ed. G. Colli and M. Montinari (de Gruyter, 1999), 87, 132.

because of the *Übermensch.* Julian Young writes, "Only the 'great' individual, the 'superman,' is of value; the rest of us must be his slaves. . . . On the Darwinian line of argument, the great individual is valuable only as a *means*, this time a means to the evolution of *society as a whole* to a 'higher' condition."[17] The means to such a society for Nietzsche is the *Übermensch*, who heralds his great personal truths and leads society on revolutionary paths. Social Darwinism was an *en vogue* theory in the late nineteenth and early twentieth centuries, and Nietzsche co-opted this theory in order to leverage a new age of humanity, values, and truths. Using Zarathustra as his European prophet, Nietzsche anticipated the social conditions were becoming more fertile for a future world flourishing with new truths, hence the term often associated with Nietzsche: perspectivalism.

Nowadays, perspectivalism (also known as perspectivism) is often misunderstood within culture and even the church. In order to understand Nietzsche's take on this topic, allow me to make a few clarifications. First, perspectivalism is often made synonymous with relativism, the belief that no absolute truths exist, and all truths are relative to persons, cultures, societies, times, and geographies. It is convenient to read Nietzsche through such a relativistic lens, but that's not what he is aiming for. To be clear, I do believe relativism (as commonly understood today) is a *reappropriation* of Nietzsche's perspectivalism in American culture. Yet, several other influences such as radical individualism, rebellion against authority, and the sexual and cultural revolutions of the American 1960s and '70s are also philosophical and cultural factors in modern discussions of relativism. Again, as noted in this book's introduction,

---

[17] Young, *Friedrich Nietzsche*, 198.

Nietzsche is often misunderstood, which leads to misappropriations and misapplications of his work in modern life. In other words, it is unfair to claim Nietzsche was an extreme relativist who held no truths at all, especially without understanding his larger philosophical project with its nuances, layers, and textures. As will be demonstrated at the end of this section, he does believe in gradations of truth, even if that truth is pragmatic, and that pragmatic truth can spawn new "higher" truths in a future society. Fundamentally, Nietzsche's perspectivalism is an exploratory notion that interweaves his thoughts on psychology (epistemology) and evolution in contrast to modernity's epistemology.[18]

As a critique of modernity's **rationalism** with its overconfidence in the mind, objectivity, and indubitable truths, Nietzsche is trying to humble European scholarship to illustrate a more honest way that is full of limitations and fallibilities.[19] Retreating into a rather modest stance, Nietzsche believes that all perspectives (ancient Greek, Christian, modern, Nietzschean) can never

---

[18] In *Beyond Good and Evil,* Nietzsche demonstrates his perspectivalism thus: "But as I say, this is interpretation, not text; and someone could come along with the opposite intention and interpretative skill who, looking at the very same nature and referring to the very same phenomena, would read out of it the ruthlessly tyrannical and unrelenting assertion of power claims. Such an interpreter would put to you the universality and unconditionality in a 'will to power' in such a way that virtually every word, even the word 'tyranny', would ultimately appear useless or at least only as a modifying, mitigating metaphor—as too human. . . . And given that he too is just interpreting—and you'll be eager to raise that objection, won't you?—then, all the better." See Nietzsche, *Beyond Good and Evil: Prelude to a Philosophy of the Future*, trans. Marion Faber (Oxford University Press, 1998), 23.

[19] For more on this topic, see Adam B. Seligman, *Modernity's Wager: Authority, the Self, and Transcendence* (Princeton University Press, 2000).

completely get outside their epistemic viewpoints and lenses.[20] They are conditioned by their viewpoints and incapable of excarnation.[21] In fact, Nietzsche considers perspectivalism to be a "condition of life" that everyone is subject to.[22] But there are questions that must be raised: Which one is the most reliable and trustworthy viewpoint? Which offers the truest picture of the world? Is there a possibility for truth in the impending Nietzschean age?

As we have already seen, Nietzsche disregards traditional takes on the world, such as the Platonic, Christian, and even early-Enlightenment viewpoints, and as noted earlier they are

---

[20] Writing on perspectivalism, relativism, and the Christian faith, philosopher Merold Westphal states, "What we must keep in mind is that to say that certain ideas, beliefs, practices, or interpretations are relative to this cultural or historical horizon is to say that they are conditioned by that context and would be different, or even impossible, in other contexts. Thus the biblical interpretations of the desert fathers are relative to their mode of monastic life. Since only God is absolute and we are relative, this kind of relativity shows up all over the place. But it is not at all the same as the relativism that says, 'Anything goes,' every interpretation is as good as every other one. To equate the two is to succumb to sloppy thinking." Merold Westphal, *Whose Community? Which Interpretation?: Philosophical Hermeneutics for the Church*, ed. James K. A. Smith (Baker Academic, 2009) 50. Additionally, pertaining to the discipline of hermeneutics (especially in the twentieth century), some may suggest that the death of God prefigured the death of the author in literary criticism, such that Roland Barth's and Stanley Fish's death of the author is a reappropriation of Nietzsche's death of God within postmodern criticism. Such a connection may have some warrant, further testifying to Nietzsche's profound impact in academia concerning truth and how truth can be known. See Anthony C. Thiselton, *Hermeneutics: An Introduction* (Eerdmans, 2009), 306–26.

[21] Borrowing from Charles Taylor, excarnation is the attempt to disembody oneself as if to get an objective, God's-eye view of the world without biases, presuppositions, or subjectivities.

[22] Nietzsche, *Thus Spake Zarathustra*, 103–6.

dismissed on the basis that they breed *décadence*; they birth death, not life. So, if every epistemic picture of the world is conditioned to one's perspective, and if traditional perspectives are degrading to life, then, Nietzsche's "claim for the will to power—his, as he sees it, [is the] corrected and completed version of Darwinian science—comprehends reality in a way that is more comprehensive and powerful than any rival theory."[23] There is a possibility for truth in his brave new world. Even if Nietzsche is self-aware that his perspective is not absolute, he still is convinced that his view is the most comprehensive and powerful because it generates life via the will to power. It is, in a sense, the most truthful explanation because it "works, which, in other words, [it] gives us power over ourselves and our environment."[24] As stated in the last chapter, personal will to power aligns oneself to the biologi cal and cosmic wills to power, therefore making it pragmatically and existentially true.

Nietzsche's Truth in the Modern Cultural Imagination

Throughout this chapter so far, I attempted to illustrate how Nietzsche understood nihilism as a historical, cultural, and philosophical idol and his unquenchable quest for new moralities, values, and truths in *Thus Spoke Zarathustra.* As noted in

---

[23] Young, *Friedrich Nietzsche*, 416.

[24] Young adds that Nietzsche's perspective is "very much like the outlook of American pragmatism (which actually has its roots in Schopenhauer's and Nietzsche's philosophy)" (*Friedrich Nietzsche*, 416). For a profound explication of Nietzsche's influence on American pragmatism, see Jennifer Ratner-Rosenhagen, *American Nietzsche: A History of an Icon and His Ideas* (University of Chicago Press, 2012).

chapter 1, modern culture has inherited and imbibed a similar social imaginary with a shared perception of trust, truth, and the quest for new values.[25] Our cultural imagination is injected with cynicism and skepticism toward sources of authority, whether they be theological, institutional, political, or religious. This is our shared reality. Suspicion is the epistemological default setting in the modern cultural imagination, an imagination haunted by **disenchantment**. One famous sociologist known for his writings on disenchantment was the German sociologist Max Weber. Categorizing Weber's views on disenchantment, Jason Ā. Josephson-Storm writes that Weber's views have become a popular mentality among Westerners on four levels:

1. *Metaphysical realism* (the belief that the world is and does not represent)
2. *Ontological homogeneity* (the belief that there are no truly extramundane objects or people)
3. *Ethical predeterminism* (that God has really decided each individual's soteriological fate) or *value nihilism* (the excision of value from the world of fact)
4. *Epistemological overconfidence* (the belief that everything can be known by means of intellectualization/theoretical rationality)[26]

---

[25] To reiterate, Taylor defines a modern social imaginary as "the way we collectively imagine, even pretheoretically, our social life in the contemporary Western world." See Charles Taylor, *Modern Social Imaginaries* (Duke University Press, 2004), 1.

[26] Jason Ā. Josephson-Storm, *The Myth of Disenchantment: Magic, Modernity, and the Birth of the Human Sciences* (University of Chicago Press, 2017), 286.

Without context these terms may be difficult to understand, so allow me to clarify while weaving this discussion of truth into the modern disenchanted imagination. First, Weber's sociological research spawned within a few decades of Nietzsche's writings and influence. As a German writer in the early twentieth century, Weber wrestles with European scholarship and their disenchantment of the world. In the writings of Immanuel Kant, Johann Wolfgang von Goethe, Arthur Schopenhauer, Nietzsche, and a host of other modern figures, Weber recognizes that the *meta* of metaphysics has been immanentized, thus leaving society with material physics alone. Corollary to the immanentizing of metaphysics, the world has become flattened—only the mundane exists, and there's nothing supernatural or extramundane in existence because God and the gods are dead or unknowable. Next, in a Weberian disenchanted world, ethics is either a matter of irrational faith (as in an extreme Calvinistic predeterminism) or ethical systems are nullified because meaning becomes a self-created value determined by the individual. And finally, disenchantment happens when everything can be truly known without faith, religion, or magic. In short, reason becomes the final source of authority, and that reason is firmly located within the individual self. Reason knows while faith believes according to a disenchanted model of modernity.

In Josephson-Storm's reading of Weber, disenchantment is another (epistemic) layer in the modern imagination, especially how modern historians and scholars have used it. Even though Josephson-Storm does not cite Nietzsche, I am arguing that Nietzsche's philosophy shapes how Americans imagine their world without metaphysics and metaethics—hence, an early form of disenchantment predicated in Nietzsche's last decade of writing. Meta-realities and meta-truths are nullified and dead, for Nietzsche. Thus, in the next century, the cultural conditions become favorable for new frontiers for what reality is and what truth is.

Many contemporary Westerners have certainly heeded Nietzsche's call to consider Zarathustra's lion spirit, the one who rejects traditional "thou oughts" and embraces the "I wills" of experimenting with self-creation and self-truths. As explained previously in this chapter, "thou oughts" are external authorities that influence or dictate behavior because of their social power. As outlined in previous chapters, Nietzsche unmasks such powers as oppressive and poisonous. These authorities, rooted in ancient Greek and Christian thought, have manmade origins, and they leverage their sociological force to empower themselves and disempower others. According to the Nietzschean psychology, God does not really exist; he is a projection of our inner selves, thus making "Truth" (absolute truths) nothing more than an absolutizing or deifying of our personal preferences.

In the modern imagination, though, Westerners have reappropriated Nietzsche's takes on truth. For instance, Americans typically do not hope for a revolutionary *Übermensch*. They are not in search for a superman figure to lead the way toward revolutions on morality and truth.[27] Nietzsche's social optimism has a bit too much aristocratic flair for America's democratic

[27] Again, I am painting with broad strokes when commenting on American culture. A case can be made, I believe, that several populations of Americans do long for a type of *Übermensch* within our political systems. Even politicians—laden within their rhetoric—portray themselves as an *Übermensch*, especially when they proselytize for a more prosperous and fertile future when the majority population puts their hope and trust in them, their politics, and their policies.

individualism. Generally speaking, most Americans truncate the *Übermensch* part of Nietzsche's future world and embrace an individual's self-making through his or her personal truths.

At a closer inspection of Nietzsche's framework, we find that Nietzsche is merely co-opting the functions and roles of Truth, absolutes, and universals for the purpose of internalizing them. He recategorizes *where* truth is. Even though his project attempts to put to death and bury old systems, Truth has not dissolved, and it has not died. It's still alive and well, and it has morphed into a Dionysian face. As the myth holds, Dionysius dies and rises a multitude of times to become something new. Likewise, says Nietzsche, former notions of Truth must die in order for rebirths of truth to become possible. In ancient Greek and Christian metaphysics, Truth was external, eternal, and universal, and Nietzsche has merely internalized Truth, deifying and absolutizing the self as Truth-maker. The self has become Self or, theologically speaking, the self has become God.

This turn inward, writes Charles Taylor, "may take us beyond the self as usually understood, to a fragmentation of experience which calls our ordinary notions of identity into question."[28] Not only are ordinary notions of identity called into question, but ordinary or traditional notions of truth are also invented. Taylor adds that these new conceptions of identity and truth are what make Nietzsche "one of the main forerunners and inspirers of twentieth-century modernism."[29] The turn inward to the self as the creative source of truth transpires a new movement within twentieth- and twenty-first century Westerners. Among a host

---

[28] Charles Taylor, *Sources of the Self: The Making of the Modern Identity* (Harvard University Press, 1989), 462.

[29] Taylor, *Sources of the Self*, 463.

of other conspirators in modernity, Nietzsche revolutionizes *how* and *where* truth is found and celebrated. No longer does the self need to look to religion or other external sources of authority; look within, says Nietzsche, and do what seems right in your own eyes.

Prophets and Proclamations: Learning How to Be Truthful

Within the larger context of biblical literature, prophets were Yahweh's representatives who corrected kings, religious leaders, and the Israelite people when the community of faith had broken covenant with Yahweh and needed to return to him. Some of the most common prophetic accusations included idolatry, forming alliances with foreign nations and their deities, and neglecting the welfare of the poor, marginalized, widow, and orphan. The basis of the prophetic message was the law, which functioned like a pedagogical guide (Gal 3:24) to Yahweh's redeemed people. Loyalty to Yahweh brought blessings, while disloyalty brought curses, as succinctly captured in Deut 28–30. In seasons of disobedience, one responsibility of the prophets was to prompt Israel toward repentance that they might submit themselves before Yahweh's covenantal faithfulness, grace, mercy, loving kindness, and justice.

The event of God's in-breaking justice is often called "the day of the Lord" in the prophets. Jeremiah, for example, focuses on God's judgment against Israel's corruption and the surrounding nations' violence, often describing this impending event in dramatic metaphors and language. This "day of the Lord" language often invokes the all too common perception that the biblical prophets are foretellers, types of divinely ordained priests who predict the future, which is partly true.[30] The biblical prophets also use poetic language to capture Yahweh's already but not yet justice that will rescue Israel from their state of disobedience, moving them from exile to freedom. Several of the prophets, such as Isaiah, expect a future restoration when both Israel and the surrounding nations will experience Yahweh's liberating redemption (Isa 53).

To summarize briefly, there are three common strands within the Hebrew prophetic literature: (1) The prophets stressed the call to covenantal faithfulness, concretely found in the law as the origin and source of its daily living. (2) Corollary to the keeping of the law, the prophets shepherded a moral imagination in the entire community of Israel, from kings to commoners, to reorder their lives into truthful and faithful living as an act of worship of Yahweh. (3) They generally predicted coming disaster based on their social, cultural, ethical, religious, and political circumstances.[31]

---

[30] Paul Copeland writes that the prophets "'predicted' the future on the basis of their exceptional insight into the signs of the times. On the other hand, this tendency also arises from an interest in the social comment of the prophets, joined to the conviction that the prophets primarily addressed the future of immediate concern to their hearers, and this is a perspective which must be appreciated. The prophets certainly did speak of the distant future, as was recognized by David in 2 Sam 7:19. Likewise, Isaiah told Hezekiah of the coming Babylonian captivity, an event 100 years in the future. However, it is worth noting that Hezekiah's response (2 Kgs 20:19) was not one of vexation for the future of the nation, but gratification that his own days would be undisturbed." Paul E. Copeland, "A Guide to the Study of the Prophets," *Themelios* 10.1 (1984): 6.

[31] These three areas are largely adapted from Abraham Heschel's *The Prophets* (HarperCollins, 2001).

As we can begin to see, Nietzsche's Zarathustra parodies Israel's prophets, divinely ordained individuals sent to prepare the people for action while longing for an immanent justice and salvation. Zarathustra stresses faithfulness to him and his message as the one who originates an in-breaking reality for all who heed his voice. Additionally, Zarathustra shepherds a particular moral imagination for Europeans to reorder their lives toward ethical individualism and perspectivalism with the hope that a new societal dawn, a "day of the Lord," might arrive through their fidelity to Zarathustra's message. Finally, Zarathustra expects a future disaster based on the *décadence* and nihilism within his present social, cultural, ethical, religious, and political age.

Acknowledging our present Nietzschean age, how can the church learn to be truthful in a post-truth world?[32] Post-truth is an attempt to live, move, and be in a culture *beyond* the Christian notions and narratives of truth. It's a mode of navigating a world that sees and senses reality without Truth, absolutes, or universals. Describing this mode of living, Charles Taylor refers to it as exclusive humanism or a "social imaginary able to account for meaning and significance without any appeal to the divine or transcendence."[33] And a social imaginary solely focused on the present, horizontal, and material world is an imaginary saturated with a disenchanted lens, as just outlined. In the process, truth becomes a sociological and psychological force because it is no

---

[32] I am borrowing this term "post-truth" from Jeffrey Dudiak. See Jeffrey Dudiak, *Post-Truth?: Facts and Faithfulness* (Wipf & Stock, 2022).

[33] James K. A. Smith, *How (Not) to Be Secular: Reading Charles Taylor* (Eerdmans, 2014), 141. In context to our conversation, Nietzsche tries to account for truth without any appeal to transcendentals, whether they be Platonic forms or thoughts in the mind of God.

longer "attached" to metaphysical or superphysical qualities and characteristics.

Truth, thus, becomes what a democracy says it is—an internal gut feeling or psychological desire.[34] As Dudiak notes, "in light of all of the confusion and ambiguity, we are tempted to trust our guts, our intuitions, our emotions, and personal preference, rather than any outside authority's attempts to provide us with the truth."[35] Obviously, Nietzsche is not the only culprit for how Westerners perceive truth in our cultural moment, yet he is one among many guilty Enlightenment conspirators who immanentizes truth—making truth merely a psychology and sociology and not a metaphysics or theology. In his schema, truth is found within and not outside of humanity.

On the one hand, Nietzsche's reconfiguring of where truth can be found should strike caution within the church. When God's people become self-reliant and disregard his authority—as found in Judg 17–21—spiritual corruption and rebellion are nearby, as captured by the phrase "there was no king in Israel; everyone did whatever seemed right to him" (Judg. 17:6; cf. 18:1; 19:1; 21:25). It is worth noting how this movement inward parallels Israel's movement away from Yahweh. In other words,

---

[34] Alasdair MacIntyre refers to this moral system as *emotivism*, which "teaches that all judgments, or more precisely all moral judgments, are merely an expression of preferences, attitudes or feelings." See Alasdair MacIntyre, *After Virtue: A Study in Moral Theory* (University of Notre Dame, 2007), 53. Such an emotivism is probably the most prevalent moral system among Americans. In fact, a pastor recently told me a story where he and a deacon were discussing a church matter. The longtime deacon told the pastor, "I know what the Bible says about this, but at the end of the day, this is how I feel about it. And my feelings are stronger than what the Bible says."

[35] Dudiak, *Post-Truth?*, 5.

Israel becomes so self-consumed and radically independent that she neglects Yahweh and his promises of shalom. On the other hand, Nietzsche captures something remarkably biblical within Zarathustra's call for faithfulness to his radical message. In short, biblical truth is closer to *embodied faithfulness* than it is to mere rightly ordered thinking—as is the moral vision of the Hebrew prophets.[36] As noted above, *to reorder one's loyalties in embodied faithfulness is essential to truthful living*.[37] Whenever Israel rebelled against Yahweh, their social, cultural, ethical, religious and political orientations were wrapped in other loyalties to foreign ideals, narratives, rituals, and gods. In so doing, their existential living was unfaithful and untruthful to the God who redeemed them. In response to this untruthful living, repentance is required—or an embodied reorientation of allegiances. Capturing this biblical sense of truth, Dudiak notes that when "the Bible speaks of truth, it is not primarily concerned with truths of fact, but with truth as faithfulness."[38] If Scripture outlines truth as fundamentally a rightly ordered way of life, an embodiment of the redemptive story, then we may be better equipped to answer the question, "How can the church learn to be truthful in a post-truth world?"

First, the church must acknowledge disenchantment as a living social imaginary of the West. As a living and active

---

[36] Instead of locating truth within the mind, Nietzsche rebels against modernity's (Cartesian) exaltation of rationalism. His rebellion likely has origins in his reading of Friedrich Hölderlin. See Sue Prideaux, *I Am Dynamite!: A Life of Nietzsche* (Duggan, 2018), 32–36.

[37] For a companion set of books that directly deal with embodied faith, loyalty, and truthful living, see Carmen Imes, *Bearing God's Name: Why Sinai Still Matters* (IVP Academic, 2019) and Imes, *Being God's Image: Why Creation Still Matters* (IVP Academic, 2023).

[38] Dudiak, *Post-Truth?*, 16.

orientation toward the world, this social imaginary pictures a flattened, horizontal, immanent, and material realm no longer haunted by myths, spirits, or a Holy Ghost. Not being attentive to this Nietzschean-inspired social imaginary can lead to a shallow cultural engagement and apologetics—a topic directly addressed in the postscript. Yet, it is worth quickly noting that some apologetic models are more sensitive to and thus more compassionately aware of another's social imaginary.[39] Being truthful, then, is neither dismissing nor degrading another's social imagination, but in and through imbibing a biblical social imaginary the church can compassionately honor the other person while also inviting him or her to consider the existential implications of staying within their disenchanted social imaginary.[40]

Second, when truth is immanentized, it becomes recategorized differently from Greco-Christian eternal language. No longer is truth associated with authorities, powers, or metaphysical realities; it is refashioned in terms of the self, emotions, and wills to power. This means that truth is synonymous with what "I feel on the inside," a further American reappropriation of Nietzsche's

---

[39] For example, some apologetic models may focus on "winning an argument" to convert the nonbeliever. Yet, such models are rarely empathetically or compassionately concerned with the human being. They are simply just trying to hurry to get their main points across. Justin Ariel Bailey's *Reimagining Apologetics* is a very helpful and holistic approach to modern apologetics. See Bailey, *Reimagining Apologetics: The Beauty of Faith in a Secular Age* (IVP Academic, 2020). Dayton Hartman and I cover a handful of apologetic models in our book, *The Pastor as Apologist: Restoring Apologetics to the Local Church* (B&H Academic, 2024).

[40] In the postscript, I will explore an apologetic model adapted from Francis Schaeffer's own apologetic approach of "taking the roof off."

will to power, where the will to power triumphs over external, traditional ideals and ideologies of truth. In his book *God and the Between*, William Desmond articulates this absolutizing of the self as a common movement among Westerners. In the modern imagination, the transcendent is neither dead nor has it disappeared but is instead renarrated. Describing this Western condition, Desmond writes, "We turn from God, turn toward ourselves as immanent transcendence, and lay hold of our own power to master the flux of equivocal transience."[41] This is the lion spirit of Nietzsche. The self is loaded with God-like "thou shalts," thus internalized into "I wills." In response, the church can consider winsome ways to illustrate how the self has been idolatrized since Nietzsche. In other words, the self has been exalted and glorified to the point where its preferences, wills, desires, and feelings have been worshipped. This should offer a conversational bridge with nonbelievers because Truth has not died but has only become deified within the self.

In summary, being truthful as the church means to embody the biblical-theological narrative of Scripture, and more specifically, it means embodying the way, the truth, and the life of Christ by being "possessed" by his Spirit in an age where spirits, ghosts, and gods are unbelievable. Moving beyond an exclusive humanistic worldview requires an openness to the possibility of transcendentals and eternals, yet the question remains: "What are the conditions for such an openness toward such a terrain, a territory beyond the physical and material?" We will hold this question for the postscript.

---

[41] William Desmond, *God and the Between* (Blackwell, 2008), 59.

Part Three

Pressures

Part 1 of this project introduced you to the life, terminology, and overall philosophical project of Nietzsche, and Part 2 acclimated you to how Nietzsche parodied the first half of the biblical narrative (Old Testament). In an Augustinian sense, he was "plundering" the Christian faith to reappropriate notions for his own ends. In Part 3, we will continue to see how Nietzsche parodies the second half of biblical narrative (New Testament). I also aim to introduce another category: pressures. This term is a truncated version of Charles Taylor's "cross pressures." In *A Secular Age*, Taylor writes, "The whole culture experiences cross pressures, between the draw of the narratives of closed immanence on one side, and the sense of their inadequacy on the other, strengthened by encounter with existing milieu of religious practice, or just by some intimations of the transcendent."[1] A merely physical immanent world leaves us unfulfilled and wanting for something more, something transcendent. In Part 3,

[1] Charles Taylor, *A Secular Age* (Harvard University Press, 2018), 595.

we will explore the theological and practical possibilities (the pressures) of a public theology in a post-Christian age, so that we further reveal the inadequacies of Nietzsche's philosophy for the modern world.

Chapter 6

The Christ and the Antichrist (On Faith)

The 2019 film *Joker* depicts Arthur Fleck's descent into madness, culminating in a chilling appearance on *Live with Murray Franklin*. As Gotham simmers with unrest and protests, Franklin, the jovial host, encounters Fleck backstage. Intrigued by the unsettling white paint adorning Fleck's face, Franklin attempts to connect, wondering aloud if it is a sign of solidarity with the city's chaos. Fleck's response is a hollow denial, a chilling declaration that he's adrift in a sea of nihilism, believing in nothing. Fleck's reply is an antinomy, an illogical conflict. To say that one does not believe anything is to believe something, and Fleck's life manifests a multitude of beliefs. He incarnates and embodies what he believes.

As will be explored in this chapter, Nietzsche contends that the true essence of redemption rests not in adopting a new faith but rather in embracing a new way of life. Nietzsche differentiated between faith and a way of life. The former, rooted in Christianity, is nothing more than a blind myth, whereas the latter affirms earthy, biological living discovered in the will to power. To his despair, the biblical-theological narrative does not differentiate between faith and a way of life. Rather, they are two sides of the same coin. Also, Nietzsche considered faith to be an oppressive, out of touch imprisonment that chains humanity to an antiquated myth. In response, Europe needed a liberator, a messiah, a christ! Throughout this chapter, we will identify the notions of faith and myth in Nietzsche's *The Anti-Christ*, which served as his last triumphant song for Europe to heed the call of true liberation from Greco-Christian ideologies. Regretfully, Nietzsche's "liberation" from faith culminates in an indentured slavery to Nietzsche's false hope. As William Desmond aptly describes, "Nietzsche felt the snap of chains, but leaves us still in chains, even as he exhorts us to lift our legs in dance."[1] Like the Joker, Nietzsche may deny faith, yet his life incarnates a faith, an embodied way of life.

This chapter has two goals. First, it will introduce Nietzsche's true messianic figure. As surveyed in previous chapters, we may suspect that his messiah was Zarathustra or even the *Übermensch*, but those are merely literary puppets for our German philosopher. Nietzsche believed that his messiah was Nietzsche himself. After concisely summarizing his work *The Anti-Christ*, we will engage with the second goal of this chapter, which is to reveal the messiah-like characteristics that Nietzsche imports on himself, especially the notion of faith in his new world order.

[1] William Desmond, *God and the Between* (Blackwell, 2008), 28.

The Anti-Christ: *Décadence* and Faith

Written in 1888, *The Anti-Christ* continues Nietzsche's philosophical project of inaugurating the new frontier of an exploratory society based on the deaths of God, metaphysics, ontology, morality, and truth. Within his opening pages, he raises this concern: "The problem I raise here is . . . what type of human being one ought to *breed*, ought to *will*, as more valuable, more worthy of life, more certain of the future."[2] Nietzsche's speculative trajectory does not waver in all his publications from the 1880s. With each work, he becomes more convinced of his project's goal and mission: To unveil Christianity's *décadence* and nihilism so that Europe can move beyond this oppressive system into a new future without its concepts, language, and practices. To reiterate, Christianity—which champions weakness—breeds death and decay. He writes, "Christianity has taken the side of everything weak, base, ill-constituted, it has made an ideal out of *opposition* to the preservation instincts of strong life; it has depraved the reason even of the intellectually strongest natures by teaching men to feel the supreme values of intellectuality as sinful, as misleading, as *temptations*."[3] Nietzsche's first opponent in *The Anti-Christ* is the theological notion referred to as "human depravity," which has been framed within the Christian tradition as a "moral accusation of man."[4] According to Nietzsche, this concept has been used by Christian theology to hold humanity back. To call a person depraved is to

---

[2] Nietzsche, *Twilight of the Idols and the Anti-Christ,* trans. R. J. Hollingdale, ed. Michael Tanner (Penguin, 1990), 128.

[3] Nietzsche, *Anti-Christ*, 129.

[4] Nietzsche, *Anti-Christ*, 129.

restrain them of their instinctual will to power. Instead, Nietzsche borrows the term depravity to turn it against Christian theology, saying, "I call an animal, a species, an individual depraved when it loses its instincts, when it chooses, when it *prefers* what is harmful to it." Nietzsche's "depravity" is anything that promotes *décadence*, a cultural disintegration or decline. In distinction to Christian *décadence*, Nietzsche writes, "I consider life itself instinct for growth, for continuance, for accumulation of forces, for *power*: where the will to power is lacking there is decline."[5]

As the previous chapters elaborated, Nietzsche proclaims his enthusiasm against Christianity because it does not promote physical, material, and organic living.[6] Christianity seems to be overly concerned about eternal ideas, metaphysical dilemmas, moral ambiguities, and salvific hopes that blind Christianity's promoters and followers to true, everyday life.[7] Nietzsche makes his stance abundantly clear:

> In Christianity neither morality nor religion come into contact with reality at any point. Nothing but imaginary

---

[5] Nietzsche, *Anti-Christ*, 129.

[6] Early in *The Anti-Christ*, Nietzsche states, "Wherever the will to power declines in any form there is every time also a physiological regression, a *décadence*" (139).

[7] Nietzsche has strong and angry words for theologians: "I make war on this theological instinct: . . . Whoever has theological blood in his veins has a wrong and dishonest attitude towards all things from the very first. . . . Wherever the influence of the theologian extends *value judgment* is stood on its head, the concepts 'true' and 'false' are necessarily reversed: that which is most harmful to life is here called 'true', that which enhances, intensifies, affirms, justifies it and causes it to triumphs is called 'false.'" See Nietzsche, *Anti-Christ*, 132. In short, Nietzsche holds that Europe must unlearn everything it has been taught about metaphysics and morality.

> *causes* ('God', 'soul', 'ego', 'spirit', 'free will'—or 'unfree will'); nothing but imaginary *effects* ('sin', 'redemption', 'grace', 'punishment', 'forgiveness of sins'). A traffic between imaginary *beings* ('God', 'spirit', 'soul'); an imaginary *natural* science (anthropocentric; complete lack of the concept of natural causes); an imaginary *psychology* (nothing but self-misunderstandings, interpretations of pleasant or unpleasant general feelings, for example the condition of the *nervus sympathicus*, with the aid of the sign-language of religio-moral idiosyncrasy—'repentance', 'sting of conscience', 'temptation by the Devil', 'the proximity of God'); an imaginary *teleology* ('the kingdom of God', 'the Last Judgment', 'eternal life').[8]

For Nietzsche, life cannot and should not be discovered in Christianity. It does not say anything remotely close to what reality is like. Ultimately, life is found in the law of evolution. Here is where Nietzsche's Darwinian proclivities of strength, power, and dominance are at odds with Christ's emphasis of weakness, humility, and servitude. When Christianity focuses on the weak, it erupts in emotional pity toward that which is weak, which "thwarts the law of evolution." Pity thus becomes a type of "practical nihilism" because pity, as an emotionally learned response (due to Christianity's power), actively hinders the evolutionary processes of a new humanity, a new society, and a new future.[9] And, Nietzsche says, the *pathos* of pity is faith.[10]

---

[8] Nietzsche, *Anti-Christ*, 137.

[9] Nietzsche, *Anti-Christ*, 130.

[10] In a letter to a friend in December 1888, Nietzsche describes *The Anti-Christ* as the "work of agitation." See Julian Young, *Friedrich*

For Nietzsche, pity is grown from the soil of faith, which he describes as a "closing [of] one's eyes with respect to oneself for good and all so as not to suffer from the sight of incurable falsity."[11] Faith, then, is an existential and epistemic blindness; like a blindfold over one's eyes, it has prevented an entire society from seeing and living into the evolutionary laws of the world. It's a denial of the psychic, organic, and cosmic wills to power inherent within the world.[12] This perspective was not uncommon in the Enlightenment. Faith was believed to hinder or prevent free inquiry, yet many figures from David Hume to Immanuel Kant considered reason, not faith, as the adjudicator of truth, thereby creating an incompatibility between faith and reason in modernity.[13] Taking an alternate route against modernity's exaltation of reason, Nietzsche sees a different incompatibility at play: between faith and the will to power.

As the previous chapters attempted to illustrate, Nietzsche articulates a psychosociological narrative of hostility between slave and master moralities, thus generating what he calls *ressentiment.* As ambassadors of the slave morality, Israel and then later the church rose to power over their nobles, indoctrinating all tribes, nations, and tongues to have faith in the gospel, a

---

Nietzsche: A Philosophical Biography (Cambridge University Press, 2010), 529. This is one of the reasons why I describe his distaste and disgust of faith as a *pathos*, because his aim was not merely a philosophical critique but an aggressive and aggravated extermination of Christianity.

[11] Nietzsche, *Anti-Christ*, 132.

[12] On these three wills to power, see chapter 2.

[13] Hence, Kant's premise in *Religion Within the Bounds of Bare Reason* and Hume's *Dialogues and Natural History of Religions.* Both publications presume reason's ability to adjudicate religion, which is a complete contrast to the millennia prior where *fides quaerens intellectum* ("faith seeks understanding").

supposed life-giving power that, for Nietzsche, ultimately generates death and *décadence*. This narrative is reiterated in *The Anti-Christ* from its origins in Israel to the New Testament and then modern Europe.[14] Nietzsche writes:

> The little rebellious movement [of Israel] which is baptized with the name of Jesus of Nazareth is the Jewish instinct *once more*—in other words the priestly instinct which can no longer endure the priest as reality, the invention of an even *more abstract* form of existence, an even *more unreal* vision of the world than one conditioned by an organized Church. Christianity *negates* the Church.[15]

Not only does Nietzsche claims that this religious imagination of Moses, Jesus, and Paul arose from within a power struggle between slave and master, but he further proposes another issue tied to the concept of faith: The Judeo-Christian religions are out

[14] Nietzsche, *Anti-Christ*, 146–83.

[15] Nietzsche, *Anti-Christ*, 151. Even though we may disagree with a large portion of Nietzsche's words here, there is an element of truth to his critique. Some forms of Christianity have negated the church. To translate, the modern American church has been guilty of abstracting doctrines like salvation, making faith into merely a matter of ideas about Jesus or abstract beliefs we hold in our heads. We might refer to this issue as a neo-Gnosticism where abstractions are glorified and particularities are degraded. A few healthy responses to this abstraction of faith and doctrine come from evangelical voices like Matthew Bates and Kevin Vanhoozer, who have proposed that faith is closer to an embodied allegiance and that doctrine is a dramatic way of life. See Bates, *Salvation by Allegiance Alone: Rethinking Faith, Works, and the Gospel of Jesus the King* (Baker Academic, 2017) and Vanhoozer, *The Drama of Doctrine: A Canonical Linguistic Approach to Christian Doctrine* (Westminster John Knox, 2005).

of touch abstractions established on violence. Thus, Nietzsche believes faith is an invented and detached power play designed to crush and persecute any outsiders. Faith, then, fails because it does not offer true deliverance but only subjugation to an ancient morality, metaphysical "truths," and an imaginary God. If this is the oppressive system that Europe is enslaved to, then who will deliver Europe from such bonds? And what is the means of salvation? In short, what is Nietzsche's notion of "faith" as the means of deliverance?

The Anti-Christian Messiah

If faith is an abstracted, out of touch orientation toward the world and a religious power play meant to dominate "pagans" and enemies, then who will deliver Europe from the claws and shadows of Christianity? Parodying the biblical arc and its concepts, Nietzsche attempts to inspire Europe to deny their faith in Jesus of Nazareth and pledge their faith in his messiah. In fact, he proposes a messiah *beyond* the Christian messiah.

As explored in the last four chapters, Nietzsche often looks beyond his present Christianized age to the horizons of his anticipated future world. The term "meta-" originates from the Greek prefix *meta*, signifying "after" or "beyond," like Nietzsche's moral hope in his title, *Beyond Good and Evil.* Nietzsche also desires to be the *anti*-Christian, the one who scornfully looks at where Europe was and is (hence, "anti-"), but also beyond (the "meta-") to expect a coming liberator. This beyondness within Nietzsche's writings comes from a place of disgust and dejection; he carries a deep disdain for European culture but remains hopeful for its future. Nietzsche wants to instill this hope because, if

Europe listens, they will experience an extraordinary change, but, like the biblical narrative, cultural and personal redemption is inaugurated through a messiah. In the remainder of this section, I want to peer behind the poetic smokescreens of Nietzsche's Zarathustra and his *Übermensch* to unveil the messiah who would pioneer a new world order, and Nietzsche was convinced he was that messiah.

To be clear, nowhere have I found a sentence penned by Nietzsche where he exclaims, "I am the liberator of Europe!" That being said, his publications from the 1880s herald a profoundly egoistic (and maybe egomaniacal) message. Being sensitive and considerate of Nietzsche's mental state, the year of 1888 is a contested one among Nietzsche scholars. There seems to be evidence of the early onsets of mania in Nietzsche's mind, and throughout 1888 he oscillates between sanity and insanity.[16] In several of his final letters to friends, he signs them as "The Crucified" and "Dionysus." It would be easy to describe these signatures as mania driven, yet it seems, as Young describes, these moments show "a certain continuity between his philosophy and his madness."[17] Possibly so. Young and I speculate on this latter point, but if Nietzsche's 1880s works are read sequentially, Nietzsche's "madness consisted in a habitation of the Dionysian state," even if it is a "confused one."[18] To put it simply, Nietzsche's ego—his fascination with himself and his philosophy—orbited around a great rescue of Europe, and as such I think it is possible that Nietzsche believed he could be Europe's messiah. This savior

---

[16] Young, *Friedrich Nietzsche*, ch. 25.

[17] Young, *Friedrich Nietzsche*, 530.

[18] Young, *Friedrich Nietzsche*, 530.

mentality is pregnant in the lucid writings of his last decade. For Nietzsche, the biblical Christ was necessary to pave the way for him, the Crucified Dionysian who would overcome death (or at least his philosophy would) in order to resurrect a new European society. Nietzsche reasoned himself to be both the Antichrist but also the meta-messiah, the one who overcomes Christ(ianity) and the one who lives beyond its deathly shadows.

Nietzsche's *Pathos* Against Faith in the Modern Cultural Imagination

As outlined previously in this chapter, Nietzsche finds himself in a difficult dilemma, a kind of philosophical impasse: He disavows Christianity while borrowing from its narrative's metaphorical concepts. This internal antimony within Nietzsche's philosophy is why I continue to use the words "plagiarizing" and "parodying" throughout this project. Nietzsche wants to annihilate anything remotely Christian while living off its conceptual bounty. He was not the only or first philosopher guilty of this inconsistency within his writings. It was an overlooked error of many philosophers in modernity. In fact, Charles Taylor captures such inconsistencies in modernity, but instead of referring to them as parodies he refers to them as being "parasitic":

Nietzsche wants to annihilate anything remotely Christian while living off its conceptual bounty.

> This self-concealing kind of philosophy is thereby parasitic. In the case of the radical Enlightenment, doubly so.

> First, it is parasitic on its adversaries for the expression of its own moral sources, its own words of power, and hence for its continuing moral force. But second, since it undermines all previous formulations of the constitutive good which could ground the life goods it recognizes, without putting any in its place, it also lives to some degree on these earlier formulations. . . . Nietzsche's challenge brought out the unavowed borrowing from Christianity that underpins this naturalist humanism and at the same time showed how vulnerable this makes it.[19]

Nietzsche clearly understood that Enlightenment and post-Enlightenment figures like Kant, Schopenhauer, and Wagner lived off the plentitude of Christianity.[20] As I have illustrated for five chapters now, Nietzsche's philosophy is parasitic as well. Even if he denies faith as an abstracted ruse that is painfully hopeful for a future heavenly world, Nietzsche himself invites Europe into a similar notion of faith where he beckons for Europe to entrust itself in his philosophical "good news" that a new world is coming, if they just trust and have faith in this message.

The 2022 film *The Whale* portrays an obese, gay teacher named Charlie (played by Brendan Frasier) who suffers chronic health issues. Realizing his debilitating health, the overarching plot follows Charlie as he tries to rekindle a relationship with his estranged daughter. Along the way, a cultish church that is seemingly invested in helping Charlie has the ulterior motive of "saving his soul." In a heart-wrenching moment of anger

---

[19] Charles Taylor, *Sources of the Self: The Making of the Modern Identity* (Harvard University Press, 1989), 339.

[20] Of the many philosophers and figures he critiques, these three are in his top five.

about his deceased boyfriend (Alan), Charlie confesses: "You think Alan died because he chose to be with me? . . . You think God turned his back on him because he and I were in love?" Commenting on this scene, Brett McCracken writes, "If Charlie is meant to be a sort of Christ figure, his gospel message is one of authenticity and 'love is love' sexual freedom. He teaches a writing class online and repeatedly tells his students to write 'honest' things. Honesty is the ultimate value in Charlie's gospel—in the 'honesty to self' sense."[21] Similarly, Nietzsche viewed the Judeo-Christian religions as disconnected from reality and built on a foundation of violence. He believed faith to be a fabricated tool of control used to oppress and exclude those who did not conform. In his view, faith ultimately fails because it offers not true liberation but instead enslavement to outdated morals, abstract "truths," and a fictional God.

At a more philosophical level, a similar narrative can be found in Western culture today with its fascination with certain variations of critical theory.[22] For instance, it is not uncommon among Westerners to attribute oppression and violence to faith. In their book *Christianity and Critical Race Theory*, Robert Chao Romero and Jeff M. Liou write:

---

[21] Brett McCracken, "Villainous Christianity in 'The Whale,' 'The Wonder,' and 'Women Talking,'" *The Gospel Coalition*, January 27, 2023, https://www.thegospelcoalition.org/article/villainous-christianity-movies/.

[22] As much as I would love to engage with critical theory in this book, I have chosen not to enter that conversation, mainly because it is beyond the argumentative and conceptual scope of this book. It is worth noting though that Nietzsche inspired many figures and institutions affiliated with critical theory. To read more on the origins of critical theory, see Carl Trueman, *To Change All Worlds: Critical Theory from Marx to Marcuse* (B&H Academic, 2024).

> When Pope Francis visited Canada in 2022, seeking repentance and reconciliation over emerging documentation of the historic abuse of the country's indigenous people, the Catholic Doctrine of Discovery was once again in the protest spotlight. The seizure of indigenous lands had been justified by the fifteenth-century doctrine, which has yet to be repealed. In most every conceivable area of social life in the United States, statistics *and* stories of the influence of race and racism abound—health outcomes, employment, housing, education, criminal justice, media representation, politics, and notably, congregational life.[23]

As evident in the storyline of *The Whale* and in Romero and Liou's quote, faith communities are more often than not perceived as oppressive and repressive within the modern cultural imagination. This perception has become deeply ingrained in the Western imagination, thus generating an emotion of angst and anger that generates the twin responses of disgust and protest—or worse, a "canceling" of such narratives, ideas, and practices. McCracken adds that some of Hollywood's narratives visually express the "larger culture's angst and grievances about Christianity," thereby aesthetically reinforcing this emotional and attitudinal response to the Christian faith.[24]

Most modern Americans may not know what critical theory is, and Samuel D. Hunter (writer of *The Whale*) may never have read Nietzsche, but they have imbibed Nietzsche's sentiment

---

[23] Robert Chao Romero and Jeff M. Liou, *Christianity and Critical Race Theory: A Faithful and Constructive Conversation* (Baker Academic, 2023), 92–93.

[24] McCracken, "Villainous Christianity."

against "singular narratives and universal truth claims, viewing them as bids for power."[25] Additionally, Americans typically "exalt lived experience and downplay objective reasoning as masculine and Eurocentric." They "view privilege as collective and rooted in oppression," and they "posit an adversarial relationship between different genders, classes, and ethnic groups."[26] Each of these categories has predominant characteristics within a modern cultural imagination. In other words, modern Americans have imbibed this *pathos* against faith as opposed to ascribing cognitively to a Nietzschean theory against faith.

Modern Americans have imbibed this *pathos* against faith as opposed to ascribing cognitively to a Nietzschean theory against faith.

This last statement further buttresses the explanatory power of Charles Taylor's epistemic model that highlights the imagination over theory-driven models. He writes, "I adopt the term imaginary (i) because my focus is on the way ordinary people 'imagine' their social surroundings, and this is often not expressed in theoretical terms, but is carried in images, stories, and legends. It is also the case that (ii) theory is often the possession of a small minority, whereas what is interesting in the social imaginary is that it is shared by large groups of people, if not the whole society."[27] Taylor's imaginary model is pre-

---

[25] Neil Shenvi and Pat Sawyer, *Critical Dilemma: The Rise of Critical Theories and Social Justice Ideology—Implications for the Church and Society* (Harvest House, 2023), 314.

[26] Shenvi and Sawyer, *Critical Dilemma*, 314.

[27] Charles Taylor, *Modern Social Imaginaries* (Duke University Press, 2004), 23.

cisely why it is acceptable to affirm two paradoxical statements: (1) Most Americans do not know who Nietzsche is, yet (2) most Americans hold a Nietzschean-inspired sentiment and narrative. Narratives evoke emotions, and such emotional irritations with faith communities have undeniably crept into the modern cultural imagination today. With this *pathos*, this aversion to faith "playing in the background" of the American imagination, how can the church respond? To be more specific, how can the church be faithful in a post-faith world?

The Spirit of Christ: Learning How to Be Faithful

Ultimately, Nietzsche wanted Europe to see faith unveiled as a detached corrupting force and to ultimately move beyond faith, subscribing to a mode of *post-faith*: a society no longer dependent upon Christianity's cultural authority and dominion. According to Taylor, in the nineteenth century, "unbelief comes of age. . . . So that for many people in many milieux in our day, [unbelief] can become a world unto itself."[28] This believability of unbelief, or what I am calling "post-faith," inspired a late twentieth-century movement called "postmodernism," and for such adherents, "The transcendent is off their map."[29] As outlined a few times in this project, many of modernity's historical figures considered religion and faith as subservient to reason, whereas Nietzsche perceived faith as out of touch with reality altogether and as both deaf and mute to the real world teeming with a will to power. If it is to be considered anything, faith is an oppressive, violent mythology contrived by certain religiosocial powers.

[28] Taylor, *Secular Age*, 374.

[29] Taylor, *Secular Age*, 374.

Obviously, the Christian faith has Jewish origins, but it is philosophically acceptable to not imagine God, as Nietzsche does, as a fictional character manufactured through a class strife between slave and master. If we are attentive to Nietzsche's psychologizing of God, we would discover that his storied explanation is itself a *mythos* (see Nietzsche's own metanarrative in chapter 1), and every *mythos* calls and beckons for allegiance, for a faith-filled giving of oneself to a story. Thus, Nietzsche wants his audience to adopt his interpretation of history as a superior *mythos*.

To tease these thoughts out a little more, Paul Ricoeur suggests that myths—including narratives, rites, and beliefs—are not fairy tales but rather are metaphorically robust and narratival ways of relating to reality.[30] And as storied creatures, human beings are personal selves who are deeply connected to a way of speaking that expresses personal and communal credos, such as "I believe in," or better, "I am faithful to." Selfhood, then, is fundamentally a lived experience of conviction rather than a certainty based on logic or science.[31]

Similar to Taylor's social imaginary, Ricoeur understands that everyone incarnates an operating *mythos*. In short, myths are not optional but are essential to being human, and to be human, says Ricoeur, is to be faithful to a story via its origins, characters, plot, ethics, tastes, meanings, purposes, metaphysics, and practices. As Ricoeur rightly posits, our identities are shaped through our allegiances, our faith in something or someone, which provokes

---

[30] Paul Ricoeur, *Interpretation Theory: Discourse and the Surplus of Meaning* (Texas Christian University Press, 1976).

[31] See Paul Ricoeur, *Oneself as Another* (University of Chicago Press, 1995).

in us certain beliefs, emotions, actions, and so forth. Nietzsche correctly illuminates the way (Christian) myths shape identity, which then affects actions and beliefs in a culture, yet Nietzsche naively assumes—like several philosophers in modernity did—that he is outside of any *mythos*, that is, some sort of compelling social imaginary carried in images, stories, and legends that shape his identity.

Nietzsche's identity is conflicted because he lives between a Christian *mythos* and a modernity *mythos*. The latter, as noted earlier, is parodying the former *mythos* in order for "the expression of its own moral sources, its own words of power, and hence for its continuing moral force."[32] Again, Nietzsche's philosophical call to move beyond this Christian *mythos* is itself the *mythos* of modernity, aligning the self to a "better" story under the banner of science, and for Nietzsche, the Darwinist notions and explanations about reality are more compelling than the Christian *mythos*. At the end of the day, Nietzsche is not beyond faith and certainly not beyond any *mythos*. As Taylor's quote noted earlier, "Nietzsche's challenge brought out the unavowed borrowing from Christianity that underpins [his] naturalist humanism."[33] But if faith is not something anyone can move *beyond* but rather something deeply human, then how can the church practice faithfulness in a supposedly post-faith age?

As teased throughout this chapter, faith has been described as an embodied way of life that shapes identity through narratives, rites, images, and beliefs (a *mythos*). The church, then, is a faith among a culture of faiths: scientisms, cults of sports, new age spiritualities, political alliances, philosophies and theories

---

[32] Taylor, *Sources of the Self*, 339.
[33] Taylor, *Sources of the Self*, 339.

on gender and identity. Recognizing that faith is an inescapable human condition, this explanation can open conversations to more meaningful and charitable dialogues about embodied living. These discussions get to the heart of identity and allegiance, and prod one's neighbor to ask not, "Do you have faith?" but rather, "What is your faith?" Or better, "Whom do you *already* serve?"[34]

Moreover, if our identities are shaped by allegiances rooted within a *mythos*, and if one's narrative identity answers many "who" questions—Who is this? Who said that? Who is that? Who are we?—then we could say that our identities are formed by faith in a "who." To be even more specific, every *mythos* has ultimate allegiances to something or someone, even a messiah-like figure. Nietzsche heralded his gospel, a good news announcement that the new European world does not need faith, and he served as this new world's messianic hope. Unquestionably, this Nietzschean *pathos* against faith has pervaded the American imagination, consequently demonstrating that Nietzsche has become a type of messianic prophet. Western society has shifted into a post-faith age where faith is seen as optional, unessential, and gratuitous.[35]

If pockets of Western culture have a *pathos* against faith, then what are some winsome and alternative ways against the tide of

---

[34] This latter question has deep resonances with Joshua's question to the Israelites as they enter into the promised land (Josh 24). It's a question that positions Israel to consider who their highest allegiances are to: the gods of the nations or Yahweh? Additionally, the question has Pauline overtones as well, where he reminds the Roman church that they are always already faithful to either death or resurrection, yet they must choose one of the two (Rom 6:6–13).

[35] The rise of the religious "nones" serves as a sociological "fact" of Nietzsche's post-faith society. See James Emery White, *The Rise of the Nones: Understanding and Reaching the Religiously Unaffiliated* (Baker, 2014).

such an animus? It would be dismissive to the conversation if the answer did not involve an incorporation of several highlighted points in this chapter. For example, part of the answer should integrate two features: first, the biblical *mythos* with its narratives, rites, symbolic images, and beliefs that, second, formatively shape a narratival identity and embodied way of life. To make these thoughts more tangible, we must acknowledge the role of the Spirit in the life of the church as the personal agent who actively (re)orients the church in allegiance to the Father and Son. Through this communion with the triune God, the church's life is realigned to the shalom-making mission of God. In so doing, the church becomes an Edenic city that possesses the qualities of God: love, joy, peace, patience, kindness, goodness, faithfulness, gentleness, and self-control (Gal 5:22–23). Through faithful alignment with the Spirit, the church establishes conditions and spaces to overcome a *pathos* of faith, or at the very least the church provides a better alternative to a Nietzschean *pathos* of faith.[36]

In conclusion, Nietzsche correctly understood that Christianity held enormous cultural influence in Europe and that there was a politics of the body at work.[37] To adopt James K. A. Smith's language, there is a *liturgical* politics of the body at work—ideas, practices, institutions, habits, and cultures that formatively prime human beings toward "certain visions of the kingdom and particular configurations of the good life."[38]

---

[36] These thoughts will be further explored in the postscript where I will submit that cultivating practices of patience are necessary for our anxious age.

[37] Here, I borrow from Leslie Paul Thiele's title, *Friedrich Nietzsche and the Politics of the Soul* (Princeton University Press, 1990).

[38] James K. A. Smith, *Desiring the Kingdom: Worship, Worldview, and Cultural Formation* (Baker Academic, 2009).

Nietzsche envisioned a post-faith society that was no longer influenced by the Christian vision of the good life. In addition, his post-faith society does not nullify faith; rather, humanity still teems with varieties of faith. This is where we feel and experience Taylor's "cross pressures," the tension between two conflicting imaginaries: the Christian, transcendent *mythos* and Nietzsche's immanent *mythos*. We still experience a pull toward transcendence, toward faith and allegiance, in Nietzsche's *mythos*, even though he denies faith. This confined and limited existence leaves us feeling unfulfilled, yearning for something greater, something that transcends our current reality.

Nietzsche envisioned a post-faith society that was no longer influenced by the Christian vision of the good life.

Agreeing with Smith, a liturgical politics of the body is evident. Nietzsche "campaigns" for the Western imagination to behold a new post-faith world on the horizon, and I am convinced that the Spirit working through the spiritual disciplines can incubate and shape the church's heart and imagination in the kingdom vision, habits, and *mythos* of Christ. I mention these concluding thoughts merely as a tease for the postscript, where I attempt to further illustrate how to overcome or out-narrate the Nietzschean *mythos* that says faith is dead. In part of that final chapter, I will suggest that the ancient practices of the church offer invaluable formative power to resituate and reorient the church to the God who defeats death.

Chapter 7

New Creations and Beyond Nietzschean Ghosts (On Hope)

Let us recap the main arguments of this project before delving into the final chapter. In Part 1, we explored some layers of the European milieu that Nietzsche wrote in and for. In Part 2, we saw how Nietzsche's engaged with some Old Testament themes and demonstrated how he parodied the first half of the biblical canon (the Old Testament). Here in Part 3, we've transitioned to the second half of the biblical canon (the New Testament) to investigate further how Nietzsche parodied biblical themes (i.e., Christ and faith) while also clarifying how Nietzsche's philosophy creates "pressures" in our modern world. This final chapter leans into some eschatological pressures of our cultural moment. Along with numerous other early modern philosophies in his day, Nietzsche proposed a secular utopia that offered promises of progress. In contrast to these utopian parodies of Scripture's new creation (Revelation 21–22), the church proclaims a far grander vision. It affirms the Christ-centered nature of reality, pointing back to a "very good" world designed by God, redeemed through

Christ, and destined for an even more glorious, "very, very good" resurrected future.

Willing a New Creation: A Nietzschean Eschatology

In each of his publications in the 1880s, Nietzsche expresses full conviction that Europe (and the West) would only experience a mammoth social renewal if it was willing to revalue its values, that is, embark upon a "transvaluation of values." As noted earlier, in 1886 Nietzsche published *Beyond Good and Evil*, a pivotal work in his project to reevaluate all values. Its subtitle, *Prelude to a Philosophy of the Future*, reveals his ambitious, future-oriented goal. As Julian Young notes, Nietzsche planned to follow *Beyond Good and Evil* with a four-volume masterpiece titled *The Will to Power: Attempt at a Revaluation of All Values*, yet his mental health rapidly declined around 1889, preventing that publication.[1] Nietzsche's transvaluation of values was a multifaceted endeavor. As we saw in chapter 3, he challenged Europe's conventional values (meaning and morality) and urged his hearers to reassess their social, cultural, and practical worth. If Europe was willing to trust Nietzsche, a new future could arrive through their reorientation to a will to power. Nietzsche's project of revaluing all values was driven by a desire to dismantle the dominant Greco-Christian framework, particularly its emphasis on ascetic

---

[1] Julian Young, *Friedrich Nietzsche: A Philosophical Biography* (Cambridge University Press, 2010), 407. The work *The Will to Power* would be posthumously published the year after Nietzsche's death by his sister and caretaker, Elisabeth Förster-Nietzsche and Peter Gast, who compiled and organized this work based on Nietzsche's notes on the topic.

"nay-saying" ideals. He believed these values denied life's inherent vitality (in exchange for a heavenly afterworld), and he sought to replace them with a life-affirming perspective that embraced a "yea-saying" earthly existence.

Until this point in this project, you may suspect that Nietzsche's philosophy erupts into a multiplicity of wills to power, each competing with one another. If that is the your suspicion, then you are correct. Nietzsche, indeed, advocated for a multiplicity of heroic and individualistic values, because a plurality of perspectives could spew limitless horizons of possibility, including incredibly fertile possibilities for new truths, morals, faiths, spiritualities, and selves (as outlined in the previous chapters). Such a warring of autonomous wills could, as one might suspect, produce violence and war. According to Nietzsche, this future world "prophesized" a thriving, flourishing European world *without violence and war*. But as he puts it, his philosophical war with Christian values and culture was a "war without gunpowder."[2] The ideal for his **eschatological** world is the proto-Greek culture (largely pre-Plato) whose festivals, poetry, theaters, and sciences were erected on creativity, exceptionality, art, and heroism. Adapting the idea from Fyodor Dostoevsky, Nietzsche believed that beauty and art would save the world, albeit through Nietzsche's symbols and story.

> Nietzsche's project of revaluing all values was driven by a desire to dismantle the dominant Greco-Christian framework, particularly its emphasis on ascetic "nay-saying" ideals.

[2] See Nietzsche, *Sämtliche Briefe: Kritische Studienausgabe*, eds. G. Colli and M. Montinari (de Gruyter, 1999), 50.

Nietzsche heralds that heroic individualism and action are the impetuses of his eschatological world. But notice, his future depends upon the will to power or an active and eager set of performances that inaugurate his anticipated world. As Young records, "The will to power remains, to the end, the governing 'principle' of *healthy* life. What really happens to it in the final works is that it is transformed from a principle of universal *explanation* into a principle of *demarcation*, demarcation between the healthy life and *décadent* life."[3] As a principle of demarcation, Nietzsche holds that the life-affirming and healthy remnant of Europe who understands him will enact his philosophy to cultivate the future world into existence. This anticipatory yet revelatory world is why I refer to Nietzsche's philosophical objective as eschatological. He both expects his impending world and attempts to inaugurate it. It is an already but not yet reality.

As one might anticipate, the use of the words "inaugurate," "eschatological," and "already but not yet" are intentional. These terms are not merely descriptive but are laden with theological meaning, reflecting core precepts of religious belief. Even though Nietzsche might detest these categories, his notions of the will to power, the self, and his future society are eschatological in nature. More pointedly, I argue that Nietzsche reinterprets (read: parodies) the biblical concept of new creation, offering a secularized vision of a transformed future world. His vision fits the eschatological categories of biblical literature rather nicely. Describing eschatology within the Gospel accounts, N. T. Wright posits:

[3] Young, *Friedrich Nietzsche*, 548.

> A new state of affairs has been brought into existence. A door has been opened that nobody can shut. Jesus is now the world's rightful Lord, and all other lords are to fall at his feet. This is an eschatological message, not in the trivial sense that it heralds the "end of the world" (whatever that might mean), but in the sense that it is about something that was supposed to happen when Israel's hopes were fulfilled; and Israel's hopes were not for the demise of the space-time universe, but for the earth to be full of God's glory. It is, however, an *inaugurated eschatological message*, claiming that this "something" has indeed happened in and through Jesus and does not yet look like what people might have imagined.[4]

Thus, Scripture speaks of an eschatological reality that (1) transcends the present state of affairs by (2) ushering in a future yet present reality (3) through a prophet-like messenger who (4) reorders society to bend toward a "not yet" city. In a similar way, Nietzsche envisions a future reality that will transcend the prevailing Christian worldview. He sought to usher in this new era, as symbolized by the "Great Noon" through the teachings of Zarathustra, who aimed to reshape society and pave the way for a transformed future. Per Nietzsche, the ideal city of the future will come through remembering those proto-Greek flourishing societies. The ultimate European city and culture depends upon the paradigm of this past archetypal city. Nietzsche's hope is both backward and forward looking. Nietzsche's *mythos* remembers a

[4] N. T. Wright, *How God Became King: The Forgotten Story of the Gospels* (HarperOne, 2012), 37–38.

once upon a time city and renders it for his happily ever after European city.

However, there is an inconsistency within Nietzsche's hope, because he does not clarify *how* a plurality of wills of power can steer and enact a future world without war and violence. As Young cleverly asks, "If the good for me is whatever fosters my kind of power, why should I not decide . . . that brutal rather than sublimated power is the thing for me?"[5] The multiplicity of conflicting self-expressions presents a challenge to societal peace. Nietzsche's self is intertwined with his will to power; to speak of one is to suppose the other. As David Deane writes, "The will-to-power comes to function as the self."[6] These competing voices and wills, arising from a basis of opposition, create states of perpetual violence, not peace. Despite his aspirations for a peaceful future, Nietzsche's emphasis on individualistic self-assertion and the will to power ultimately paves the way for social and cultural disorder. The self alone, via one's will to power, provides the means of inaugurating Nietzsche's eschatological city.

Despite his aspirations for a peaceful future, Nietzsche's emphasis on individualistic self-assertion and the will to power ultimately paves the way for social and cultural disorder.

[5] Young, *Friedrich Nietzsche*, 549.

[6] David Deane, *Nietzsche and Theology: Nietzschean Thought in Christological Anthropology*, Routledge New Critical Thinking in Religion, Theology, and Biblical Studies (Routledge, 2006), 48.

Nietzsche's Eschatological Cities in the Modern Cultural Imagination

Enlightenment-era political theorists, such as Thomas Hobbes and Baruch Spinoza, ran into a similar issue as Nietzsche. In their respective ways, Hobbes and Spinoza aimed to create a (future) city of hope through atomized, subjective wills. With millions of selves bumping into one another within a society, Hobbes, Spinoza, and Nietzsche each tried in their own ways to reconcile this autonomous plurality with the utopian goal of world peace and flourishing. Commenting on Hobbes and Spinoza, yet also directly applicable to Nietzsche, Graham Ward writes: "These characteristics [of plurality of atomized selves] combine to create a certain kind of space: a space for the operation of the subjective will. It will become an increasingly godless space, occupied with the Promethean task of saving humanity by human means alone. It is within this space that the modern city of eternal aspiration is constructed."[7] Within this embodied space, each person acts in accordance with his or her hedonistic desires, offering disruptive and discordant visions of any future utopian world. In this manner, Nietzsche's philosophy of hope for fresh possibilities eventually matures into an eroticization of the self in the twentieth and twenty-first centuries.

In the past century alone, Western culture—especially in America—has responded to Nietzsche's rejection of the Christian worldview with acclamation. As surveyed in *On the Genealogy of Morals*, Nietzsche denounces certain ascetic ideals of Christianity, particularly certain restrictions on physical pleasure because these asceticisms degrade the physical and devalue

[7] Graham Ward, *Cities of God* (Routledge, 2000), 137.

the body. Within *Genealogy of Morals*, Nietzsche does not reject all asceticisms. As someone who prizes self-discipline, Nietzsche believed that certain asceticisms can be helpful for striving for something more and greater (read: *becoming* who one is). However, he criticizes Christian ascetic ideals when they deny his version of flourishing and lead to nihilism and *décadence*—both of these being denials of one's present, earthly living.

From a cinematic perspective, the 2007 film *No Country for Old Men*—based on Cormac McCarthy's 2005 novel of the same name—grapples with Nietzschean themes of power, a questioning of traditional morality, and the (future) meaning of life. Situated in 1980s southwest Texas, the film narrates a long cat and mouse pursuit between Llewelyn Moss (Josh Brolin) and a sociopathic killer, Anton Chigurh (Javier Bardem). Moss, who has stumbled onto a murderous scene between drug gangs, takes the two million dollars he discovers at the scene, expecting no one to witness his silent theft. But the skilled killer Chigurh hunts down Moss to retrieve the cartel's money, and he brutally massacres anyone who stands in his way. Oftentimes, Chigurh leaves the fate of a person's life in the odds of coin flip.[8] Hunting down the hunter, Sheriff Bell (Tommy Lee Jones) attempts to thwart Chigurh's plan. Whether one encounters this story by reading Cormac McCarthy's novel or watching its film adaptation, both mediums portray Chigurh as personifying absolute power.

No Country for Old Men echoes the Nietzschean push and pull of questioning traditional morals through the hands of absolute will to power. At the end of the film, Sheriff Bell speaks of

[8] Life is meaningless, so why not entrust it to a random coin flip?

two dreams, and it is the second that prods the audience to reflect more deeply. Bell narrates that he remembers a former age when the world was simpler and when the notions of "good" and "evil" were more defined and distinguishable. But with time and age, the world, he suspects, has become grayer and more ambiguous. *No Country for Old Men* does not look back nostalgically at the past. Instead, it sees the present age with its own set of challenges and moral complexities, without suggesting that things were inherently better in earlier times. Through its metaphorical and visual images, the book and film both subtly suggest that the challenges and complexities they depict will persist into the very near future.

Now, at the musical and lyrical level, John Lennon's "Imagine" perfectly illustrates Nietzsche's secularized "new creation." In his song, Lennon invites the listener to imagine a world without both God and religion, one where citizenship is labeled by a brotherhood of humanity where there are no possessions and a communal sharing of the world. Lennon dreams of a world to come yet still out of reach, and through the death of religion and the brotherhood of man, humans can begin to fashion this world into being.

Generally speaking, this Nietzschean *pathos* has sparked a cultural rebellion in the West, further intensifying Nietzsche's petition to erupt a cultural revolution in the face of Greco-Christian morality. His critique of these "nay-saying" asceticisms has been embraced and transformed into a justification for the pursuit of sensual gratification. As authentic and genuine as Lennon may appear, his utopian vision neglects the hubristic pursuits of humanity. Ultimately, through these personal and self-serving pursuits, the new frontier of Nietzsche's future city does not resemble Lennon's eschatological city. Rather, it culminates into eschatological sites of narcissism and hedonism, as depicted in *No Country for Old Men*. Nietzsche's "new creation" comes through erotic and self-indulgent experiments, and through these experiments, a new self is (perpetually) born based on one's preferential *eros*. More importantly, identities are shaped (and reshaped) via these experimentations, thereby creating a citizenship unified under the banners of performance, will to power, and self-expressive autonomy.

Nietzsche's Eschatological Age: Learning How to Be Hopeful

To reiterate one main point of this chapter, Nietzsche envisioned an eschatological reality that would transcend his present. He sought to usher in this new era through a prophetic figure who would reorient society toward a future aligned with his own values, effectively offering a secularized version of biblical eschatology. In each chapter, I have tried to illustrate how Nietzsche parodies the biblical-theological arc of Scripture from creation to new creation. Additionally, I have argued in this chapter that Nietzsche's "new creation" is an ongoing process of self-discovery and reinvention (a *becoming* of what one is) fueled by passionate experimentation. Through these experiences, individuals continually redefine themselves, shaping and reshaping their identities according to their deepest desires driven by the will to power. Following Carl Trueman's methodological advice given in this book's introduction, the church should not depend upon cultural and "worldly" narratives and tools to understand our world (such as Nietzsche's or Lennon's hopeful secular eschatologies).[9] Instead, the church can lean into and be enlivened by the resurrected Christ, who is "the beginning, the firstborn from the dead" (Col 1:18).

As Wright exhibited in the middle of this chapter, in and through Jesus's resurrection a "new state of affairs has been brought into existence. A door has been opened that nobody can shut."[10] The current Nietzschean state of affairs "promotes a materialism which is soulless, aggressive, nonchalant and nihilistic."[11] In contrast, Jesus's state of affairs promotes an incarnational way of being that is soulful, peaceful, and meaningful because the incarnation and resurrection of Jesus both affirms creational goodness and transforms it toward its eschatological end: a new creation without death, decay, and *décadence* (Rev 21:22–27).

As has been repeated throughout this project, we live in Nietzsche's eschatological age where his ghost continues to haunt the halls of our homes, businesses, classrooms, social media, economies, marketplaces, and social imaginaries. Those who constitute the church, as players in God's resurrected drama, have been chosen by the Father not to participate in the ghostly appearances of Nietzsche in our cultural moment but instead to partake in the Holy Ghost of Christ (1 Pet 2:9). John Barclay writes regarding Paul's discussion of the body in Romans, "The body is, for Paul, the site where the 'I' is expressed and enacted; Paul's commitment to the notion of the 'resurrected body' (8:11;

---

[9] Carl Trueman, *To Change All Worlds: Critical Theory from Marx to Marcuse* (B&H Academic, 2024), 227.

[10] Wright, *How God Became King*, 38.

[11] John Milbank, Catherine Pickstock, and Graham Ward, introduction to *Radical Orthodoxy: A New Theology*, ed. John Milbank, Catherine Pickstock, and Graham Ward (Routledge, 1999), 1.

cf. 1 Cor 15:42–44) suggests that the self cannot be operative or communicative in any other way. If so, the body is the place where the resurrection life of Jesus (the new self) becomes visible and active in human lives."[12] The Spirit—as a transcending gift within the immanent—guides, directs, and empowers the church both now and in the world to come (Rom 8:11).

[12] John M. G. Barclay, *Paul and the Gift* (Eerdmans, 2015), 503.

Postscript

(Re)discovering the God Who Was Dead

So what now? In this project's introduction, I told the story about teaching Nietzsche to my college philosophy class. After discussing this German philosopher for a few weeks, I asked my students, "What if Nietzsche was right? Or what if Nietzsche was even partly correct, how would it change the way you lived in and experienced the world?" As you have discovered throughout this book, I firmly believe that Westerners continue to live in the shadow of Nietzsche; he continues to exert enormous cultural influence and authority in our daily lives—in our con-

Westerners continue to live in the shadow of Nietzsche; he continues to exert enormous cultural influence and authority in our daily lives—in our conversations on theology, identity, meaning and morality, truth, faith, power, and hope.

versations on theology, identity, meaning and morality, truth, faith, power, and hope.

After attempting to demonstrate to those college students that some of Nietzsche's ideas still haunt many of our institutions, disciplines, topics, cultural ideologies, and the like, one of my students—in a moment of humble transparency—asked, "So what now?" Professors love questions like these. She is right: If Nietzsche has shifted Western culture in a new direction with his writings, how do we respond? To be more specific, how do we as *the church* respond? To be fair, this postscript is exploratory in nature regarding that question. Recognizing our cultural moment with its Nietzschean affinities, I am nevertheless hopeful for how the church can charitably, wisely, winsomely, and missionally navigate our Nietzschean age through a robust Christian public theology.

Toward a Public Theology for our Nietzschean Age

When Nietzsche penned his works in the 1870s and '80s, he wrote from the cultural margins. He was a minority voice in a day where Christendom still cast a long shadow. Nietzsche's writings sounded extremely heretical on the ears of many of his contemporary readers.[1] Now that Nietzsche's Great Noon has nearly arrived, the shadow is cast in the opposite direction. In our Nietzschean age to write from a Christian perspective is to

---

[1] Jennifer Ratner-Rosenhagen documents how Nietzsche was first received as an extreme thinker in America in *American Nietzsche: A History of an Icon and His Ideas* (University of Chicago Press, 2012), 210–17. Regarding his reception in Europe, see Rüdiger Safranski, *Nietzsche: A Philosophical Biography*, trans. Shelley Frisch (Norton, 2002), 317–50.

already speak from the margins. But I do not identify this marginalization as either despairing or a cultural war to fight. In the closing sections of each previous chapter, I tried to illustrate how to do public theology in conversation with the relevant topics engaged therein (e.g., theology, identity, morality and meaning, truth, faith, hope). As noted in the introduction, my aim throughout this work has been to explore creative ways for the church to engage charitably, wisely, winsomely, and missionally with Nietzschean-inspired topics. Those four adjectives are defining pillars for a public theology.

First, at their best *public theologies are to be charitable*. As noted in the introduction, charity not only seeks out the Other but also seeks the well-being of the Other. A public theology sees cultural ideologies as more than abstract concepts; they are embodied in people, our neighbors with their lives, homes, communities, and stories. "To know is a relational engagement. It is a communal task of care; as such, charity ought to be the foundation."[2] Thus, charitable public theologies demonstrate love for one's neighbor by seeking his or her flourishing.

Also, *public theologies are to be wise*. They are to begin with "the fear of the Lord" (Prov 1:7), because fear (read: reverential awe) postures the church to see Christ as the "hidden wisdom" (1 Cor 2:7) that unveils the mysteries of God's created order. Hence, "in the search for wisdom, fearing the Lord thus involves both the starting point of the journey and the *foundation*, or ground, on which a life of wisdom is built."[3] Beginning with doxological

---

[2] Alexander Sosler, "Prodigal Love and a Hermeneutic of Charity: How Grace Changes Learning," *Pro Rege* 48.3 (2020): 23–28.

[3] Craig Bartholomew and Ryan O'Dowd, *Old Testament Wisdom Literature: A Theological Introduction* (IVP Academic, 2011), 80.

reverence, our public theologies acknowledge our creatureliness and ignorance to seek Christ as the one who gives wisdom "generously and ungrudgingly" (Jas 1:5).

Next, *public theologies are to be winsome*. In embodying the gospel of Jesus in the first century, the early church was endearing, engaging, and appealing. On Mars Hill, Paul did not throw philosophical grenades at his Athenian hearers. In engaging with the Epicurean and Stoic philosophers around him, he quotes the philosopher-poet Epimenides and the didactic poet Aratus to demonstrate winsomely his familiarity with those classical authors in order to invite the Epicureans and Stoics into a better way (Acts 17:16–34).[4] Correctly understood, Jesus's gospel is itself beautiful, good, and true, thereby making it winsome and appealing.

Finally, *public theologies are missional*. All public theologies are contextualized theologies, because language is "always particular and traditioned."[5] As particular and traditioned acts, public theologies herald the symbols and stories of Scripture in the warp and woof of our everyday contexts, such as our homes, streets, neighborhoods, and offices. "Evangelical theology," writes Kevin Vanhoozer, "deals not with disparate bits of ideas and information but with divine doings—with the all-embracing cosmic drama that displays the entrances and exodus of God."[6] To embody and employ these theologies is to participate publicly in and perform Jesus's gospel, and they do so missionally.

---

[4] See Jonathan T. Pennington, *Jesus the Great Philosopher: Rediscovering the Wisdom Needed for the Good Life* (Brazos, 2020).

[5] John Milbank, *The Word Made Strange: Theology, Language, Culture* (Wiley-Blackwell, 1997), 29.

[6] Kevin Vanhoozer, *The Drama of Doctrine: A Canonical Linguistic Approach to Christian Theology* (Westminster John Knox, 2005), 3.

A couple of final words on public theology before exploring some practical applications in the remainder of this postscript. Ultimately, a public theology draws its lifeblood from Scripture, acting with conviction to offer alternative narratives to prevailing cultural stories, like Nietzsche's. A healthy public theology seeks to situate ideological narratives within the more compelling narrative of Scripture.[7] Considering that many Christians, especially pastors and laypersons, feel unequipped to engage with imperative cultural topics, robust and erudite public theologies can serve as helpful resources.

Through its stories, poetry, lamentations, apocalypses, songs, wisdom literature, gospel accounts, and letters, Scripture heralds a subversive paradigm for our public theologies. We could even boldly proclaim that Scripture has an underlying critical method against the principalities and powers of today's cultural ideas, ideologies, and narratives. "All Scripture," Paul writes to Timothy, "is inspired by God and is profitable for teaching, for rebuking, for correcting, for training in righteousness, so that the man of God may be complete, equipped for every good work" (2 Tim 3:16–17). As a subversive yet sufficient authoritative script, the Bible discloses a metaphysical and moral critique of both past and present cultural philosophies. In many ways, David deSilva's words regarding revelation are applicable to the entire Bible: Scripture functions as a revelatory critique of

---

[7] This echoes Chris Watkin's definition of out-narration: "Out-narrating is not about telling the better story in the sense of being the most gripping or necessarily satisfying; it is about telling the bigger story, the story within which all other stories find their place." See Christopher Watkin, *Biblical Critical Theory: How the Bible's Unfolding Story Makes Sense of Modern Life and Culture* (Zondervan Academic, 2022), 21.

"subculture's ideologies and the religiously constructed self and roles it promotes. A critical perspective requires that we examine this tendency as well, and choose what stance we will take and what practices we will adopt on the basis of what promotes the integrity of our lives rather than the perpetuation of social constructions."[8] Scripture provides a critical apparatus and mode for engaging with various ideologies. This project has attempted to demonstrate that Nietzsche's philosophy is not exempt from this critique, and that the biblical tradition offers a more compelling response to his challenges.

(Re)discovering God: What Now?

Returning to the question introduced at the beginning of this postscript, what do we do now? As Nietzsche rightly understood, if God is dead, then everything else falls with his death: metaphysics, morality, ontology, meaning, truth, faith, and hope. Each of these topics (among many others) are contingent upon God's existence. If he is dead, we can potentially establish a new society based on novel ideas, philosophies, gods, meanings, identities, and so forth. And as I have tried to demonstrate throughout this book, Nietzsche's philosophical project has persuaded some Westerners to take up his battle cry *Écrasez l'inflâme!* "Crush the infamy!" That is, crush those Greco-Christian idols that have erected a society bowing its knees to the gods of death and *décadence*. Thus, a great skepticism has pervaded the modern Western imagination, a worldview suspect of God's existence. We have lost him, in some sense, so how can we (re)discover this supposedly

[8] David deSilva, *Seeing Things John's Way: The Rhetoric of the Book of Revelation* (Westminster John Knox, 2009), 336.

dead God? Because if he is real, if he does exist, then, contrary to Nietzsche, everything matters: Theology, identity, meaning and morality, truth, faith, and hope all matter.

In the previous paragraph, I used the word "(re)discover" purposely. In his book *Cosmic Connections*, Charles Taylor explores several poets as case studies within the disenchantment of the Romantic period. Noting how the post-Romantic poetry attempted to "(re-)connect" humanity to an enchanted, divine world, Taylor writes:

> A central theme of my discussion of post-Romantic poetry has been (re-)connection. The prefix "re" here reflects the sense of loss and then rediscovery. The loss came with the uncertainty about, and growing loss of confident contact with, traditional and Renaissance notions of cosmic order: the Great Chain of Being, the Creation as a communication from God, the Kabbalah, and the like.[9]

I wish to borrow Taylor's use of the prefix "re" considering our present conversation. Through Nietzsche, Western culture has lost something important, or dare I say *essential* to its existence and flourishing, which is the reality of God. Considering this loss, we must (re)discover a deep and abiding connection with the triune God and his cosmic order. In so doing, we can retrieve and reconnect with something transcendent in the Taylorian sense. Yet, we might ask, "How is this (re)discovery possible? How can we live both in between and beyond the Nietzschean structures of immanence toward something transcendent?" The

[9] Charles Taylor, *Cosmic Connections: Poetry in the Age of Disenchantment* (Harvard University Press, 2024), 252.

answer, I suspect, lies within a passive rather than active mode of life. In the sections below, I will first describe why a winsome public theology is necessary for our Nietzschean age and then explore particular Christian modes of living as counternarratives to this Nietzschean age. As will be seen, these modes include gathered and scattered worship as well as apologetics. I am convinced that gathered and scattered worship are spiritual incubators for apologetic witness in a Nietzschean immanent frame.

> Through Nietzsche, Western culture has lost something important, or dare I say *essential* to its existence and flourishing, which is the reality of God.

Transcendent Worship Within an Immanent Frame

"My prayers feel like a bunch of jumbled words that only touch the ceiling." That was the confession of a dear friend of mine speaking about how she understood her prayer life. I've had numerous conversations like this over the years. It's a common perception among Americans to ask, "Are my prayers being heard?" This perception indicates the (epistemic) presence of an immanent frame, which is, as a reminder, "a constructed social space that frames our lives entirely within a natural (rather than supernatural) order."[10] A Nietzschean-inspired post-faith age sees transcendence under a lens of suspicion. God is dead, so prayer is ineffectual. Imagining the world via an immanent frame means "unbelief" seems to be the default setting, and faith is redundant

---

[10] James K. A. Smith, *How (Not) to Be Secular: Reading Charles Taylor* (Eerdmans, 2014), 140.

and superfluous. Why? Only the material, immanent, horizontal plane matters. Belief in God seems unimaginable, which means confession as a verbal communication with God is an incompetent act; it's seen as nothing more than a jumbling of words that bounce off ceilings.

Yet, within worship, confession as a liturgical act presumes not only God's real presence but also his greatness. It is an act of adoration of a great God who forgives his people, and confession *liturgically assumes* the greatness and grace of this God when the church speaks to him. Writing on confession, Nicholas Wolterstorff states, "We discover . . . an understanding of God implicit in this liturgical act [of confession]." In confession, God is "vulnerable to be wronged but [also] that God has in fact been wronged."[11] Thus, within worship God is presumed to be a real person who experiences relational and emotional tensions. Confession, then, intimates the reality of transcendence, or at least a plausible sphere *beyond* material, immanent, and horizontal spheres.

Confession hints at something greater, more graceful, and higher than this present world. These hints of transcendence offer a "sense that there is some good higher than, beyond human flourishing. . . . This notion of a higher good as attainable by us could only make sense in the context of belief in a higher power, the transcendent God of faith which appears in many definitions of religion."[12] Confession reveals a divine person who pursues humanity for their flourishing. Contrary to Nietzsche, there are cracks in the immanent frame where the light of

---

[11] Nicholas Wolterstorff, *The God We Worship: An Exploration of Liturgical Theology* (Eerdmans, 2015), 164.

[12] Charles Taylor, *A Secular Age* (Harvard University Press, 2007), 19.

transcendence shines through, but this divine transcendence cannot be grasped through human ingenuity, power, or sheer will. As discussed throughout this book, Nietzsche was attempting to both affirm this immanent life and grasp for some enhanced life beyond the present through human ingenuity, power, and will. "The Nietzschean understanding of enhanced life, which can fully affirm itself, also in a sense takes us beyond life; and in this it is analogous with other religious notions of enhanced life (like the New Testament's 'eternal life')."[13] Contrary to this Nietzschean vision of enhanced or eternal life, the redemptive narrative of Scripture heralds a transcendence tabernacling with humanity and its immanence.[14]

Much of contemporary American culture is fixated on discovering oneself through performance, action, and self-help. We may wrongly suspect that these active modes are *the* means of (re)discovering God. Contrarily, there may be a better way, a more favorable mode that acknowledges our contingency and creatureliness, and this mode of being comes by *passively* responding to the Otherness of the triune God, as opposed to reaching out and *actively* grasping for him through our liturgical performances and grit.

Confession is the passive means of receiving and living into the life of this transcendent, Otherly, triune God. Wolterstorff writes that confession "assumes that God will listen. It's a cry

---

[13] Taylor, *Secular Age*, 373.

[14] The entire biblical canon testifies to a God who "comes down" to meet with his people from Gen 3:8 to Lev 1:1 to John 1:14–15 to Rev 21:2–4. One major and undeniable theme of Scripture is the fellowship of God with humanity. For a work on this topic, see G. K. Beale, *The Temple and Church's Mission: A Biblical Theology of the Dwelling Place of God* (IVP Academic, 2004).

for God to hear. Another reason the church believes that it is not presumptuous for us to address God is that it believes that God has invited us to do so."[15] Confession is the response to such an invitation. When the people of God gather to confess—individually and collectively—the church is reordering its passions, desires, inclinations, and imagination to receive passively the grace and goodness of God. In and through confession, the church responds to the holy justice of the Father discovered in the person of his Son through his Spirit. In confession, Andrew Root writes, the self confesses itself as *not* magnificent.[16] As a corollary, then, the church liturgically heralds through confession that Nietzsche's merely immanent frame is fragile and that a divine transcendence demolishes his false idols of individualism and will to power.

In summary, confession is an invitation of God to receive passively God's abiding grace. Root notes, "When this transcendence breaks upon the self, the self can only receive it as a gift, a promise, a judgment, and an invitation. This inbreaking transcendence . . . can only be encountered in surrender and confession."[17] To be clear, confession is not the only conduit of grace within worship, yet it is a tangible embodiment of such an encounter of transcendence within the immanent frame. Nietzsche longed for this present life to be enhanced, and as I am trying to demonstrate, gathered worship—especially confession—conditions a hospitable space for enhanced or eternal transcendent life to

---

[15] Wolterstorff, *God We Worship*, 80.

[16] Andrew Root, *The Church in an Age of Secular Mysticisms: Why Spiritualities Without God Fail to Transform Us* (Baker Academic, 2023), 111.

[17] Root, *Secular Mysticisms*, 76.

meet with humanity, so that true spiritual, tactile, bodily, affective, and cultural flourishing can erupt within the horizontal, immanent plane.[18]

Spiritual Formation Within an Immanent Frame

Moving beyond gathered worship to scattered worship, I want to suggest in this section some ways the church can be discipled into (re)discovering God within an immanent frame. To be frank, we have absorbed a Nietzschean-inspired narrative and framework in our American culture, thereby supplementing how we imagine and orient ourselves in the Western world. Our conversations about theology, identity, meaning, morality, truth, faith, power, and hope are influenced by Nietzsche. As Justin Ariel Bailey states, "This is because our habits go deeper than our critical intellect. . . . We consume culture in ways that fit our narrative identities, the stories we tell ourselves about ourselves."[19] A hope for the church, then, is to enable the biblical-theological narrative to reshape our identities, and one avenue for such an aim is through spiritual formation.

American culture is not without its own ritualed and formative practices—its own shaping of identity via cultural habits.

---

[18] As a reminder, Jesus describes eternal life as a communal, intimate knowing of the Father as revealed through the Son (John 17:3). To tease this out more, the incarnation of God could be explained as the theological marriage of transcendence and imminence—that we "come to know" (Greek: *ginōskō*, John 17:3) the transcendent God via the imminence of his enfleshment.

[19] Justin Ariel Bailey, *Interpreting Your World: Five Lenses for Engaging Theology and Culture* (Baker Academic, 2022), 12.

Tara Isabella Burton documents a range of cultural practices that shape our social imaginary and identities:

> If you've ever been to a yoga studio or a CrossFit class, ever practiced "self-care" with a ten-step Korean beauty routine or a Gwyneth Paltrow–sanctioned juice cleanse, . . . ever compared your spiritual outlook to a Dungeons and Dragons classification ("lawful good, chaotic evil") or your personal temperament to that of a Hogwarts house, ever channeled your sense of cosmic purpose into a social justice activism, or ever tried to "bio-hack" yourself or used a meditation app like Headspace, ever negotiated "personal relationship rules" . . . with a partner, ever cleansed your house with sage, or ever been wary of a person's "toxic energy," you've participated in some of these trends.[20]

The modern world is not without its own magical incantations, self-induced happiness, and forms of religion. Each of these cultural rituals form types of knowers, and as Root correctly posits, the modern self is a performing self whose "longed-for magnificence" and identity is expressed through uniqueness.[21] This magnificence and identity is formed through ritualed cultural practices, and these sets of practices are Nietzschean inspired because they long for uniqueness, authentic identity, and individual expressivism. They ingrain within the self a notion of self-discovery *beyond* who one is or, as Nietzsche might say, "a becoming what one is" (see chapter 2).

---

[20] Tara Isabella Burton, *Strange Rites: New Religions for a Godless World* (Public Affairs, 2020), 10–11.

[21] Root, *Secular Mysticisms*, 29.

Beyond gathered worship, the church can be further shaped through an ordered set of habits aimed at formation into the image of Christ. These ordered habits are referred to as the spiritual disciplines, and the process of this maturation is called spiritual formation. One spiritual disciplines specialist, Dallas Willard, has defined spiritual formation as "the process of transformation of the inmost dimension of the human being, the heart, which is the same as the spirit or will. It is being formed (really, transformed) in such a way that its natural expression comes to be the deeds of Christ done in the power of Christ."[22] The conduit of spiritual formation comes through biblical and ecclesial practices and rituals, and this ritualed life hones the church's life toward knowing God rightly: "The Hebrew Bible and Christian Scriptures presume a thoroughly *ritualed* life for the sake of knowing correctly."[23] For the church, a symphony of authoritative and authorized practices orient and direct it toward knowing the Father and the Son via the work of the Spirit.[24]

---

[22] Dallas Willard, "Spiritual Formation: What It Is, and How It Is Done," Dallas Willard Ministries, https://dwillard.org/resources/articles/spiritual-formation-what-it-is-and-how-it-is-done.

[23] Dru Johnson, *Scripture's Knowing: A Companion to Biblical Epistemology* (Cascade, 2015), 65.

[24] A couple of clarifiers: First, since orthodox Christianity encompasses several dogmatic confessions, I use the word "symphonic" to capture the multitude of traditions and voices that uniformly herald first-order doctrines of the Christian faith. For a thoughtful work on first, second, and tertiary doctrines, see Gavin Ortland, *Finding the Right Hills to Die On: The Case for Theological Triage* (Crossway, 2020). Second, each orthodox Christian tradition may entertain distinct spiritual disciplines, yet it's fair to say that these practices carry certain levels or grades of authority for those traditions, such as *The Book of Common Prayer* for Anglicans and Presbyterians versus Baptists. And as

These robust "rites produce a certain kind of knower"[25]—a disciple apprenticed to the person of Jesus. And thus, the end (*telos*) of the spiritual disciplines is knowing the triune God, and ritualed practices cultivate an intimate nexus between earthly imminence and divine transcendence.[26]

For instance, a daily reciting of the morning and evening prayers from *The Book of Common Prayer* is one way for our social imaginaries to be formed into the likeness of Christ. Not only do the morning and evening prayers reposition the heart under the banner of the triune God, but they also invite the church into incarnating the kingdom of God, thus relocating the self in a biblical-theological narrative via embodied, Christian practices. Hence, conversations orbiting around theology, identity, meaning, morality, truth, faith, power, and hope are recalibrated when we humbly whisper:

> Almighty and most merciful Father,
> we have erred, and strayed from thy ways like lost sheep.
> We have followed too much the devices and desires
> of our own hearts.
> We have offended against thy holy laws.
> We have left undone those things

---

authoritative practices, they function as authorized rites and practices that generate spiritual formation for such traditioned communities. For more on authority and tradition, see Yves Congar, *The Meaning of Tradition* (Ignatius, 2004).

[25] Johnson, *Scripture's Knowing*, 76.

[26] For an introductory work on the spiritual disciplines that uses the metaphor of "channels" instead of "conduit," see David Mathis, *Habits of Grace: Enjoying Jesus Through the Spiritual Disciplines* (Crossway, 2016).

which we ought to have done;
and we have done those things
which we ought not to have done.[27]

Humbly posturing ourselves as we confess these words, our imaginations are baptized by the Spirit to see the world teeming with God, the one who is not dead, but the one who resurrects the dead.

Similar to the last section, I suggest that gathered worship—especially confession—offers fertile liturgical grounds for passively receiving the grace and presence of God in Christ's Spirit. Actively and willfully grasping for grace contradicts the biblical narrative, because it reveals a God who graciously and kindly reveals himself. Mastering God is reconcilable for the narrative of modernity but irreconcilable for the narrative of Scripture (see Gen 11:1–9). Thus, the spiritual disciplines are not a means of grasping after or mastering God. Rather, they are generative means of drawing near to the presence of God. Contrary to Nietzschean-inspired cultural stories and practices, which center the self and absolutize it for the goal of discovering oneself,[28] I submit that we can only discover ourselves—via

[27] See "General Confession to be said of the whole Congregation after the Minister, all kneeling" in *The Book of Common Prayer.*

[28] This cultural message of "doing to become" is powerfully captured in the film *Passengers*, featuring Chris Pratt and Jennifer Lawrence. On an interstellar spaceship traveling 120 years to a second earth, Homestead II, Jim Preston (Pratt) is awakened by a technical malfunction, and later, in a desperate and depressing moment of weakness, he awakens fellow passenger Aurora (Lawrence). Later, we discover that Aurora left Earth because she was searching for meaning and truth. Watching old videos of her friends before she departed Earth thirty years prior, one of her friends speaks these words to Aurora: "I

practices and rituals—by being known by the triune God.[29] To adapt René Descartes's famous dictum ("I think, therefore I am"), the church confesses her truest identity with the words "I am loved, therefore I am."

A Christian Apologetic for a Nietzschean Age

To reiterate, this postscript's emphasis has been to develop some constructive and creative pathways for how the church can charitably, wisely, winsomely, and missionally navigate its Nietzschean-inspired age. In the previous sections, I drew a few blueprints for how the church can map some reflective practices in gathered and scattered worship for the reformation of the ecclesial imagination, so it can contest Nietzschean symbols, narratives, and ideologies intertwined in American culture. These sections also dealt with the spiritual development of the Christian and the church—for both the individual and the community. This spiritual development is necessary in a post-faith age, because it recaptures a Christian vision where character formation is more than a personal, self-consumed interest. Rather, it is a political act, an apologetic, and even a public theology. It is an embodiment of the Petrine invitation for the church to be "ready at any

---

hope you finally find someone who fills your heart, and I hope you let him in. I hope you realize you don't have to do something amazing to be happy." Her friend's advice is a poetic summation of this entire chapter: Only through surrender can humanity discover something transcendent, something transformational.

[29] Not only is this a conclusion found in the biblical canon, but it also deeply resonates with Augustine's *Confessions* where he repeatedly intimates in his work that to know oneself is to be known by God. A modern Jewish equivalent would be Martin Buber's *I and Thou*.

time to give a defense to anyone who asks you for a reason for the hope that is in you" (1 Pet 3:15).

In the rest of this chapter, I want to display (contrary to Nietzsche) some of the ways the Christian faith is not an otherworldly and "nay-saying" religion. A healthy hermeneutic of Scripture does not agree with Nietzsche that the Christian faith says "no!" to earthly, immanent matters. Nietzsche was primarily responding to revivalist movements occurring on the continent when he vehemently wrote against Christianity. Such pietistic and Lutheran traditions were hotbeds for revivalistic fervor, where preaching about salvation and the afterlife were key themes. To respond to Nietzsche and to some "nay-saying" Christian denominations and traditions that overstress an ethereal afterlife as the *telos* of Christianity, my aim in this last section is to equip the church methodologically and practically with some charitable and winsome apologetic approaches for our Nietzschean age.[30]

In their book *The Augustine Way*, Joshua Chatraw and Mark Allen constructively critique modern apologetic models as overemphasizing thinking and believing. They write, "Modern classical and evidential apologists are prone to attend to people

---

[30] Here I am reminded of N. T. Wright's critique of such gnostic-like doctrines and traditions: "Salvation, then, is not 'going to heaven' but 'being raised to life in God's new heaven and new earth.' But as soon as we put it like this we realize that the New Testament is full of hints, indications, and downright assertions that this salvation isn't just something we have to wait for in the long-distance future. We can enjoy it here and now (always partially, of course, since we all still have to die), genuinely anticipating in the present what is to come in the future." See Wright, *Surprised by Hope: Rethinking Heaven, the Resurrection, and the Mission of the Church* (HarperCollins, 2009), 198.

primarily as *thinkers*. . . . Presuppositional apologetics tends toward engaging people primarily as *believers*."[31] Both of these approaches heavily focus on the mind, yet, according to Chatraw and Allen, where is the heart in this anthropology? Developing a fleshier theological anthropology, Chatraw and Allen contend that apologetics must also consider the "importance of humans as doxological creatures."[32] As they put it, "How we reason impacts what we worship. What we worship impacts what we believe. What we believe shapes how we reason and worship, and so on. The feedback loop is an inescapable dynamic of human cognition and decision-making." Understanding this "feedback loop" greatly affects where apologetics begins and why it is important to the present conversation. A fuller theological anthropology that includes worship, belief, and thinking is necessary in our Nietzschean age. For instance, if most Westerners consider faith as an optional ornament to add to one's living (i.e., "post-faith"), then how can the apologetic discussion begin? If many Westerners consider truth as either dead or entirely subjective, then how can the apologetic discussion begin? Finally and rather daringly, could we commence an apologetic conversation *assuming* a Nietzschean immanent frame?[33]

Rather than assuming faith, belief, or truth as optional, why not open with a stronger and more existential set of questions, such as: "What do you love?" "Do you think what you love affects

---

[31] Joshua D. Chatraw and Mark D. Allen, *The Augustine Way: Retrieving a Vision for the Church's Apologetic Witness* (Baker Academic, 2023), 54–55.

[32] Chatraw and Allen, *Augustine Way*, 54.

[33] A short and excellent work that assumes an immanent frame while providing a robust Christian apologetic is Jeffrey Dudiak's *Post-Truth?: Facts and Faithfulness* (Wipf & Stock, 2022).

your identity?" "How does your identity reveal what you love?" "How do the things or persons you love give you meaning?" "Is there a connection between our moralities and our loves?"[34] These types of questions practice a more holistic integration of what it means to be human, considering the *whole* person and not just his or her disconnected ideas or beliefs on a given topic.

When we affirm the entire humanness of a person—with all her desires, wants, beliefs, ideas, hatreds, and passions—we invite her to see the connections between worship (desire), belief, and thinking. As Chatraw and Allen write:

> The unified nature of the three aspects of humanity means that we have an opening for apologetics: engaging over the central pursuits of our shared existence as worshiping beings, which includes such experiences as our quest for meaning, our need for an identity, our longing for communal devotion, our yearning for happiness, and our desire to love and be loved.[35]

The twentieth-century pastor, theologian, and apologist Francis Schaeffer has referred to this apologetic approach as "taking the roof off." Ahead of his time, Schaeffer recognized that every person has desires, yearnings, and stories as whole human beings. They were not merely thinking things but also fundamentally doxological creatures who resonated with and longed for transcendence. Speaking of his method, he writes: "But if we do not take sufficient time to take the roof off, the twentieth-century

---

[34] A more modern masterpiece that interweaves morality and love is Martha Nussbaum's *Love's Knowledge: Essays on Philosophy and Literature* (Oxford University Press, 1992).

[35] Chatraw and Allen, *Augustine Way*, 54.

man will not comprehend what we are trying to communicate, either what his death is caused by, or the solution. We must never forget that the first part of the gospel is not 'Accept Christ as Savior' but 'God is there.'"[36] Schaeffer taps into humanity's yearning for transcendence, and his apologetic approach teases his hearers to recognize that a God is already there. In his day, as in ours, the notions of "judgment and hell are nonsense," because of Nietzsche's influence (and that of many others), which has conditioned Westerners to view and live in a world without the lenses of Christianity—or any other faith.[37] Nietzsche prompted European society to see the world with a new dictionary and through a new narrative, and his influence shaped the Western social imaginary accordingly. As a philosopher, Schaeffer acknowledges that the modern social imaginary is quickly becoming "post-Christian," and yet, despite its moving away from Christianity's lexicon and narrative, Westerners have continued to parody the Christian redemptive narrative, much like Nietzsche did.[38] "To take the roof off," then, is a necessary apologetic exercise for Schaeffer, because it invites in the "truth of the external world and the truth of what man himself is." Faulty roofs or beliefs succumb to the "blows of the real world, both internal and external," thus revealing to the human their existential confusion and despair.[39] Such an approach does not stop there though; there is good news too.

---

[36] Francis Schaeffer, *The God Who Is There* (InterVarsity, 2020), 156.

[37] Schaeffer, *God Who Is There*, 156.

[38] Schaeffer writes, "We of the West may not be brainwashed by our State, but we are brainwashed by our culture." See Schaeffer, *God Who Is There*, 156–57.

[39] Schaeffer, *God Who Is There*, 156.

The apologetic approaches of Chatraw, Allen, and Schaeffer take seriously a Nietzschean **exclusive humanism**, which, according to Charles Taylor, is the way modern Westerners imagine their world without superstitions, magic, religion, or transcendence.[40] This discloses a post-faith imagination where stories, symbols, and practices are exclusive to an immanent human plane of existence. Borrowing from Augustine's anthropology, Chatraw and Allen submit, "A person reasons with their visions of the good and the beautiful directed toward the earthly city or the heavenly city." Reasoning, or imagining, is fundamentally "connected to love and telos."[41] Public theologies, like those of Chatraw, Allen, and Schaeffer, demonstrate in their respective ways that there are *cracks in the secular* and that the light of transcendence continues to glow within immanent human planes, and one apologetic goal is to unveil these prisms of transcendence within immanence. To answer these Nietzschean-inspired imaginations in our modern world, then, God, metaphysics, and truth are not dead but rather are presently haunting the existential chambers of bodies, beliefs, stories, symbols, and cultural imaginations.

Culture Parodies Christ: A Wise Yet Winsome Mode for Public Theology

As this work has attempted to demonstrate, Nietzsche consistently parodies the Christian narrative to construct his own *mythos*. It is a post-Enlightenment story with new gods (Dionysius), a new humanity (a human becoming), a new metaphysic (a cold immanence), a new fall (*décadence*), a new set of prophetic proclamations

[40] Taylor, *Secular Age*, 222.

[41] Chatraw and Allen, *Augustine Way*, 93.

(Zarathustra), and a savior (the *Übermensch*). Nietzsche aims to establish a new society and humanity free from the influence of Christianity, yet he appropriates the biblical narrative structure (creation-fall-redemption-new creation) and vocabulary to build this future world.

At the end of each chapter, I tried to elucidate how the modern social imaginary is still seduced by Nietzsche's narrative and ideas on topics like theology, identity, meaning, morality, truth, faith, and hope. Hence, not only was Nietzsche parodying the Christian redemptive narrative, but American (sub)cultures continue to parody the themes, topics, ideas, narratives, and symbols of Scripture. As noted throughout this chapter, there *continues* to be cracks in our secular age. Consequently, if the transcendence shines through these immanent cracks, then it affords the church fertile apologetic opportunities. In other words, the "Culture Parodies Christ" option mentioned at the start of this book offers the church a wise yet winsome mode of being "salt and light" (Matt 5:13–16).

The term "mode" is an intentionally loaded philosophical term that remembers and reiterates the work of Herman Dooyeweerd, who constructed a philosophical framework referred to as "modal law-sphere theory."[42] Exploring the layers of everyday existence, Dooyeweerd postulated that reality comprised fifteen spheres or modes of existence.[43] Each of these modes of existence was con-

[42] A great introduction to Dooyeweerd is D. F. M. Strauss, *The Philosophy of Herman Dooyeweerd* (Paideia, 2021).

[43] These include numerical, spatial, kinematic, physical, organic, psychical, logical, historical, lingual, social, economic, aesthetic, legal, moral, and certitudinal. Although important, these modes are secondary to the present discussion and will not be discussed.

structed by the triune God for his image bearers to reflect and refract him. Dooyeweerd wrote:

> God has not abandoned His Creation to the spirit of apostacy. The Creation is His. It is subject to His absolute sovereignty. For that reason, the central dynamic grip of the Word of God affects not only the personal life of the Christian, nor only the church as an institutional fellowship, but all human social relationships, politics, culture, science, and philosophy.[44]

One of the callings of the church, Dooyeweerd suggests, is to acknowledge the "apostasies" or the philosophical and theological perversions of God's created order with all of its modes. In each of these modes, the church is called out to disrobe such apostasies—like Nietzschean values on truth (Col 2:14–15)[45]—and through its being, the church suggests that truth is not a hegemonic, domineering power play but a reality that participates in the life and being of God, who invites humanity to embody his truth via allegiance (faith). Through allegiance to this God, the Spirit empowers the church to be weak. The Spirit

---

[44] Herman Dooyeweerd, "Christian Philosophy: An Exploration," in *Christian Philosophy and the Meaning of History*, vol. B13 in *The Collected Works of Herman Dooyeweerd* (Paideia, 2013), 2.

[45] In Col 2:14–15, Paul demonstrates that the cross "disarms" or better "disrobes" (from the Greek word, *apekduomai*, meaning "to unclothe") the Jewish and Roman rulers and authorities who crucified Jesus. I am suggesting the church retains this cruciform paradigm in its public theology by "unclothing" and thereby "exposing" modern cultural philosophies. For this unclothing metaphor in relation to these verses in Colossians, see G. H. P. Thompson, *The Letters of Paul to the Ephesians to the Colossians and to Philemon*, Cambridge Bible Commentary (Cambridge University Press, 1967), 144.

does not create warriors, "strong men, [or] masters . . . [who are] violent in act and gesture," heralds Nietzsche.[46] The church's power as weakness may seem foolish to the cultural spheres of "relationships, politics, culture, science, and philosophy," yet power as weakness seems thoroughly Christological for Paul: "God has chosen what is weak in the world to shame the strong" (1 Cor 1:27).[47] Again, the church must decline the Nietzschean forbidden fruit that continues to tempt us to gain absolute, God-like power.

Furthermore, when the church and its members participate in the life in the Spirit, they become imitators of Christ who exemplified "love, joy, peace, patience, kindness, goodness, faithfulness, gentleness, and self-control" (Gal 5:22–23). To connect the points between this paragraph and the last one, Paul understood that the "power of the Spirit is inseparable from the power of the cross."[48] This means that the "Spirit of power is the Spirit of weakness, the Spirit of the cross."[49] Thus, the church must lean into the Spirit of weakness and the cross, who will generate love, patience, kindness, and gentleness when the

---

[46] William Shirer quotes Nietzsche's *On the Genealogy of Morals* in his *The Rise and Fall of the Third Reich: A History of Nazi Germany* (Simon & Schuster, 2011), 126.

[47] Here, I am reminded of Elon Musk's post (@elonmusk), "Unless there is more bravery to stand up for what is fair and right, Christianity will perish," Twitter (now X), July 27, 2024, https://x.com/elonmusk/status/1817273263761817710. Musk's assumptions are: (1) The strong and the powerful change culture; and (2) weakness leads to death. Ironically, dozens of Christian leaders agreed with Musk by reposting him.

[48] Michael J. Gorman, *Cruciformity: Paul's Narrative Spirituality of the Cross* (Eerdmans, 2021), 59.

[49] Gorman, *Cruciformity*, 60.

cultural *pathos* is agitated, angry, and hurt by Christianity. In so doing, the church does not embody an arrogant spirit of power as dominance, but a cruciform Spirit of humble sacrifice through compassionate listening and radically generous hospitality—in *every* mode of life.[50]

In and through a cruciform public theology, the church speaks from the margins, from the shadows of our Nietzschean age, in order to demonstrate that God is not dead and that the resurrected Jesus nourishes the existential hungering of Americans who are deeply dissatisfied and restless with Nietzschean-inspired ideas and narratives. The church intimates that rest can be found not through self-discovery, performances, or expressive identities but through a public theology that Christ is risen, and Nietzsche is not.

---

[50] Check out Seth Freeman's thoughtful article on tangibly embodying this Spirit for political seasons: "How to Talk About God and Politics in Polarized Times," *Christianity Today*, September 9, 2024, https://www.christianitytoday.com/2024/09/how-to-talk-about-god-and-politics-in-polarized-times/.

ACKNOWLEDGMENTS

There are so many to thank, and I have the unfortunate task of limiting myself. First off, this project would never have come to fruition without the B&H Academic team: Madison Trammel, Jessi Wallace, Logan Pyron, Kristen Padilla, Renée Chavez, Rebecca Pickard, Dakota Rice, Emily Lambright, and Kristen Ingebretson. Indeed, they are more than my fellow colleagues; they have also been incredible encouragers as this project grew from a dream into the tangible work currently in your hands. I am incredibly grateful for their insightful commentary, design creativity, marketing *savoir-faire*, and publishing expertise. I look forward to many more projects with them.

Additionally, this work was birthed from the womb of numerous philosophy and theology classes while attending Southeastern Baptist Theological Seminary. Professors such as Heath Thomas, Jeremy Evans, Bruce Little, Mark Liederbach, Bruce Ashford, Nathan Finn, Ken Keathley, Joshua Waggener, and Benjamin Quinn invested hours toward my spiritual and academic formation. In their classrooms, intellectual honesty and excellence were both highly valued and instilled within their students, and for over a decade I was a fortune benefactor of their investments. In all transparency, I see this work as a "sacrifice" in their honor.

The last acknowledgement is tailored to my bride, Jade. In the early years of our dating, I told her, "It seems Christ is calling me to do more for him." She replied, "Sounds like you need to go to seminary." At that time, I had no clue what seminary was, but she was exactly right. Then and now, she is a spiritual compass in my life.

GLOSSARY

Autonomy: In many writings of the Enlightenment age, autonomy was a prized theme. Broadly speaking, it refers to the self-governance and self-determination of the self to freely choose, think, and believe as he/she determines. Drawing from the spirit of the Enlightenment, Nietzsche advances a hyper-individuality where self-governance, self-determination, and individual freedom become resonating themes in his later writings. He promoted the notion that Europe needed an authentic, free-spirited individual to rise up and become the ideal of creative autonomy—resembling personas like Napoleon Bonaparte.

Critical Theory: Originating in the Frankfurt School, this theory is a social and philosophical approach that critiques and challenges power structures, social inequalities, and cultural norms. Often drawing from Marxist and Freudian themes, critical theory aims to uncover hidden biases and assumptions that perpetuate oppression, advocating for social change toward liberation and a more just society.

***Décadence*:** Nietzsche used *décadence* to describe what he saw as the decline and degeneration of culture and values, particularly in nineteenth-century Europe. He associated it with nihilism, pessimism, and a weakening of the will to power, often blaming

Christian morality and other life-denying philosophies for fostering this cultural and social decay.

Disenchantment: Max Weber's term, "disenchantment," describes the process in modernity where the world loses its magical, mystical, and religious significance as science and rationality gain dominance. This leads to a more efficient and predictable world, but also one potentially devoid of inherent meaning, leaving individuals to create their own values in a "disenchanted" reality.

Dionysius/Dionysian: Dionysus was more than a Greek mythological god. For Nietzsche, Dionysus functions as a philosophical psyche or even a way of being for Nietzsche's present and impending world. Dionysus represents the primal, instinctual, and chaotic forces of life, embodying passion, intoxication, and the dissolution of boundaries. He stands in contrast to Apollo, the god of order and reason. For Nietzsche, embracing the Dionysian is crucial for a full affirmation of life and the creation of new values.

Epistemology/Epistemic: Western epistemology is a branch of philosophy that investigates the nature, origin, and limits of human knowledge. It grapples with questions like: What is knowledge? How do we acquire it? How do we know that we know? What are the criteria for epistemic justification? Major epistemological theories include rationalism, empiricism, and skepticism, each offering different accounts of knowledge.

Eschatology/Eschatological: Eschatology is the study of "last things," including beliefs about the conclusion of the present era, the climax of human history, and the ultimate destiny of the world. For Nietzsche, he expects his philosophy to erect a new social order, and as illustrated in my project, his new social order is thus eschatological in nature, thereby parodying the biblical narrative of the "things to come."

Essentialism: With its roots in Plato and Aristotle, essentialism asks simply, "What makes a thing essential? What is its indestructible and inherent nature or essence?" Plato and Aristotle probed everyday objects and persons with these questions in order to understand the nature of the universe. Attempting to move beyond Plato and Aristotle's questions, Nietzsche wishes to put to death such antiquated questions to explore new philosophical territories, which has significant impact on disciplines after Nietzsche, such as science, racial theory, and gender studies.

Expressivism: Alasdair MacIntyre uses "expressivism" to describe the modern tendency to view moral statements as mere expressions of personal feelings or preferences, rather than objective truths. He argues that this emotivist approach (a rationality based on emotions) has led to a shattering of moral discourse and the loss of a shared ethical vision and framework for western society.

Eternal Recurrence/Eternal Return: Nietzsche's eternal recurrence seems to be his thought experiment that the universe, and every event within it, will recur infinitely in the same sequence. It's a test of one's affirmation of life by asking, "Could you wholeheartedly embrace this idea, including all the pain and joy, and will it to repeat eternally?"

Exclusive Humanism: Charles Taylor describes this term as a social imaginary, or a way of seeing and sensing the world with meaning and significance yet without any appeal to God, the divine, or transcendent categories.

Geist: This term was not creepy, eerie, or haunting for Europeans. Rather, it was primarily (but not solely) used to describe the intellectual and cultural movements within Europe—whether they be institutional, collective, social, philosophical, economic, or individual movements. In my book, I am using it likewise, as an intellectual and cultural "spirit of an age."

The Great Noon: In a few of his later writings, Nietzsche uses this term to describe an impending time. This epoch or age would shadow the old Greco-Christian epoch that is passing away where the future to come would bring about a revaluation and a transvaluation of values. Nietzsche believed his philosophy would stimulate the Great Noon so that Europe could seize an opportune time for cultural flourishing.

Hermeneutics/Hermeneutical: Primarily understood as a theory of interpretation, hermeneutics was a growing and thriving discipline in German scholarship during Nietzsche's time. Hermeneutics, specifically understood, applies to a reading/interpreting of texts, whereas, in broader categories, it can apply to the "reading" or interpreting of the world. Many of Nietzsche's writings on interpretation would be adopted by French philosophers, like Jacques Derrida, who entertained hermeneutics in both senses of the term: an interpretation of both texts and the world.

Ideology: This term must be understood more broadly than a set of conceptual ideas. Nietzsche's *Twilight of the Idols* is a critique of what he saw as false idols, or ideologies, in Western philosophy and culture, including traditional morality, metaphysics, and prominent thinkers. He uses aphorisms and rhetoric to "philosophize with a hammer," smashing these idols/ideologies to pave the way for new, life-affirming values. Agreeing with Nietzsche, ideologies are closer to idealized narratives of a society.

Immanent Frame/Immanentism: Charles Taylor's "immanent frame" defines the modern context in which we experience reality as a self-sufficient, natural order without reference to the transcendent. This closed framework makes belief in God optional and emphasizes secular explanations, creating a "buffered" self (read: a close mindedness), distinct from the "porous" (read: an open-mindedness) self of premodern times.

Metaethics: Whereas the discipline of ethics deals with questions like, "Is it morally wrong to steal", metaethics asks, "What do we mean by 'wrong'?" In other words, metaethics isn't about what's right or wrong. Rather, it delves into the very nature of morality itself.

Metaphysics: Simply put, it is the study and discourse of a *super*-natural reality beyond physical reality. Western metaphysics is a branch of philosophy exploring fundamental questions about reality, existence, being, time, and space. It investigates concepts beyond the physical world, such as the nature of consciousness, causality, and the relationship between mind and matter. Key figures include Plato, Aristotle, Descartes, and Kant, each offering unique metaphysical systems.

Modern Social Imaginary: A modern social imaginary is the shared, often implicit, understanding of how we collectively exist and relate in society. It's the background framework of assumptions, values, and norms that shape our common practices and sense of legitimacy, making social life possible and providing a sense of shared identity.

Moral Relativism: According to this perspective, there are no universal moral truths; what's considered right or wrong depends on the specific context, making moral judgments subjective rather than objectively true or false. This notion is opposed to moral objectivism.

Methodological Naturalism: Methodological naturalism is a philosophical approach in science that restricts explanations to natural causes and processes, excluding supernatural or spiritual factors. It doesn't necessarily deny the possibility of the supernatural but insists that science, by its nature, only investigates the observable, testable, and measurable world.

Nihilism: Nihilism is a complicated idea in Nietzsche's work, but at its core, it involves a complete rejection of value and meaning in life. Interestingly, Nietzsche believed that the very forces that traditionally claimed to offer meaning—namely, ancient Greek philosophy, Judaism, and Christianity—were actually the biggest contributors to nihilism. Why? Because, as discussed in this project, these systems promoted ways of understanding the world (metaphysics) and ways of behaving (morality) that were fundamentally opposed to life and our true nature. For Nietzsche, our true nature is driven by what he called the "will to power." Nietzsche argued that traditional values, by denying or suppressing our natural drives and promoting an "otherworldly" focus, ultimately led to the feeling that life itself is meaningless.

Ontology: Ontology is a branch of philosophy that studies the nature of being, existence, and reality. It explores fundamental questions like: "What exists? What categories of things exist, and how are they related? What does it mean for something to exist?" It seeks to categorize and understand the basic building blocks of reality.

Perspectivalism/Perspectivism: Nietzsche's perspectivism argues that all knowledge is interpreted from a particular perspective, influenced by individual drives and biases. There is no objective, viewpoint-independent truth, only interpretations. This does not mean "anything goes" but that we must be aware of the limitations and influences of our perspectives when assessing truth claims.

Rationalism: Enlightenment rationalism was a philosophical movement emphasizing reason as the primary source of knowledge and authority. It championed logic, scientific inquiry, and individual liberty, while rejecting dogma and tradition. Thinkers like Immanuel Kant and René Descartes believed that through rational thought, humanity could achieve progress, understand the universe, and improve society.

Ressentiment: Nietzsche's ressentiment describes a psychological state of suppressed anger, envy, and impotence projected outward as moral condemnation. A resentful individual, unable to express their will to power directly, inverts values, deeming their own weakness as "good" and the strength of others as "evil." It is a key component in his critique of slave morality.

Transvaluation/Transvaluing of Values: Nietzsche's "transvaluation of values" calls for a radical reevaluation of prevailing moral norms, particularly those rooted in the Jewish and Christian traditions. He believed these values suppressed the will to power and advocated for a new set of values that affirmed life, strength, and individual excellence, effectively overturning the existing moral hierarchy.

Will to Power: Nietzsche's will to power is the fundamental driving force in all living beings, a striving not just for survival but for growth, dominance, and self-overcoming. It's not merely a desire for power over others but a broader will to become more, to expand influence, and to shape the world.

Zarathustra: Nietzsche's Zarathustra is a prophet-like figure in his book, *Thus Spoke Zarathustra*. He descends from a mountain solitude to share his wisdom, proclaiming the death of God, the concept of the Übermensch, and the eternal recurrence. He serves as Nietzsche's mouthpiece for critiquing traditional values and advocating for a new philosophy.

GENERAL INDEX

SCRIPTURE INDEX

Acts

Romans

1 Corinthians

Galatians

Colossians

2 Timothy

James

1 Peter

2 Peter

1 John

Revelation